THE TRAGICALL HISTORIE OF

Hamlet
Prince of Denmarke

 HARVESTER WHEATSHEAF

New York London Toronto Sydney Tokyo Singapore

THE TRAGICALL HISTORIE OF

Hamlet
Prince of Denmarke

EDITED AND INTRODUCED BY
GRAHAM HOLDERNESS AND BRYAN LOUGHREY

HARVESTER WHEATSHEAF

First published 1992 by
Harvester Wheatsheaf,
Campus 400, Maylands Avenue
Hemel Hempstead
Hertfordshire HP2 7EZ
A division of
Simon & Schuster International Group

Designed by Geoff Green

Typeset in 11pt Bembo
by Photoprint, Torquay, Devon

Printed and bound in Great Britain by
Billing and Sons Ltd, Worcester

British Library Cataloguing in Publication Data

A catalogue record for this book
is available from the British Library.

ISBN   0–7450–1099–7 (hbk)
ISBN   0–7450–1100–4 (pbk)

1   2   3   4   5   96   95   94   93   92

Contents

General Introduction

T H I S series puts into circulation single annotated editions of early modern play-texts whose literary and theatrical histories have been overshadowed by editorial practices dominant since the eighteenth century.

The vast majority of Shakespeare's modern readership encounters his works initially through the standard modernised editions of the major publishing houses, whose texts form the basis of innumerable playhouse productions and classroom discussions. While these textualisations vary considerably in terms of approach and detail, the overwhelming impression they foster is not of diversity but uniformity: the same plays are reprinted in virtually identical words, within a ubiquitous, standardised format. Cumulatively, such texts serve to constitute and define a particular model of Shakespeare's work, conjuring up a body of writing which is given and stable, handed down by the author like holy writ. But the canonical status of these received texts is ultimately dependent not upon a divine creator, but upon those editorial mediations (rendered opaque by the discursive authority of the very texts they ostensibly serve) that shape the manner in which Shakespeare's works are produced and reproduced within contemporary culture.

Many modern readers of Shakespeare, lulled by long-established editorial traditions into an implicit confidence in the object of their attention, probably have little idea of what a sixteenth-century printed play-text actually looked like. Confronted with an example, she or he could be forgiven for recoiling before the intimidating display of linguistic and visual strangeness – antique type, non-standardised spelling, archaic orthographic conventions, unfamiliar and irregular speech prefixes, oddly placed stage directions, and

General Introduction

possibly an absence of Act and scene divisions. 'It looks more like Chaucer than Shakespeare,' observed one student presented with a facsimile of an Elizabethan text, neatly calling attention to the peculiar elisions through which Shakespeare is accepted as modern, while Chaucer is categorised as ancient. A student reading Chaucer in a modern translation knows that the text is a contemporary version, not a historical document. But the modern translations of Shakespeare which almost universally pass as accurate and authentic representations of an original – the standard editions – offer themselves as simultaneously historical document and accessible modern version – like a tidily restored ancient building.

The earliest versions of Shakespeare's works existed in plural and contested forms. Some nineteen of those plays modern scholars now attribute to Shakespeare (together with the non-dramatic verse) appeared in cheap quarto format during his life, their theatrical provenance clearly marked by an emphasis upon the companies who owned and produced the plays rather than the author.[1] Where rival quartos of a play were printed, these could contrast starkly: the second quarto of *Hamlet* (1604), for example, is almost double the length of its first quarto (1603) predecessor and renames many of the leading characters. In 1623, Shakespeare's colleagues Heminges and Condell brought out posthumously the prestigious and expensive First Folio, the earliest collected edition of his dramatic works. This included major works, such as *Macbeth*, *Antony and Cleopatra*, and *The Tempest* which had never before been published. It also contained versions of those plays, with the exception of *Pericles*, which had earlier appeared in quarto, versions which in some cases differ so markedly from their notional predecessors for them to be regarded not simply as variants of a single work, but as discrete textualisations independently framed within a complex and diversified project of cultural production; perhaps, even, in some senses, as separate plays. In the case of *Hamlet*, for example, the Folio includes some eighty lines which are not to be found in the second quarto, yet omits a fragment of around 230 lines which includes Hamlet's final soliloquy,[2] and far greater differences exist between certain other pairings.

This relatively fluid textual situation continued throughout the seventeenth century. Quartos of individual plays continued to appear sporadically, usually amended reprints of earlier editions, but occasionally introducing new works, such as the first publication of Shakespeare and Fletcher's *The Two Noble Kinsmen* (1634), a play which was perhaps excluded from the Folio on the basis of its collaborative status.[3] The title of another work written in collaboration with Fletcher, *Cardenio*, was entered on the Stationer's Register of 1653, but it appears not to have been published and the play is now lost. The First Folio proved a commercial success and was reprinted in 1632, although again amended in detail. In 1663, a third edition appeared which assigned to Shakespeare *Pericles* and six other plays which are now generally regarded as apocryphal: *The London Prodigall*, *Locrine*, *The Yorkshire Tragedy*, *Sir John Oldcastle*, *The Puritan*, and *Thomas Lord Cromwell*. These attributions, moreover, were accepted uncritically by the 1685 Fourth Folio.

The assumptions underlying seventeenth-century editorial practice, particularly the emphasis that the latest edition corrects and subsumes all earlier editions, is rarely explicitly stated. It is graphically illustrated, though, by the Bodleian Library's decision to sell off as surplus to requirements the copy of the First Folio it had acquired in 1623 as soon as the enlarged 1663 edition came into its possession.[4] Eighteenth-century editors continued to work within this tradition. Rowe set his illustrated critical edition from the 1685 Fourth Folio, introducing further emendations and modernisations. Alexander Pope used Rowe as the basis of his own text, but he 'corrected' this liberally, partly on the basis of variants contained with the twenty-eight quartos he catalogued but more often relying on his own intuitive judgement, maintaining that he was merely 'restoring' Shakespeare to an original purity which had been lost through 'arbitrary Additions, Expunctions, Transpositions of scenes and lines, Confusions of Characters and Persons, wrong application of Speeches, corruptions of innumerable passages'[5] introduced by actors. Although eighteenth-century editors disagreed fiercely over the principles of their task, all of them concurred in finding corruption at every point of textual transmission (and in Capell's case, composition), and sought the restoration of a perceived poetic genius: for Theobald, Warburton, Johnson and Steevens, 'The multiple sources of corruption justified editorial intervention; in principle at least, the edition that had received the most editorial attention, the most recent edition, was the purest because the most purified.'[6]

This conception of the editorial function was decisively challenged in theory and practice by Edmund Malone, who substituted the principles of archaeology for those of evolution. For Malone, there could be only one role for an editor: to determine what Shakespeare himself had written. Those texts which were closest to Shakespeare in time were therefore the only true authority; the accretions from editorial interference in the years which followed the publication of the First Folio and early quartos had to be stripped away to recover the original. Authenticity, that is, was to be based on restoration understood not as improvement but as rediscovery. The methodology thus offered the possibility that the canon of Shakespeare's works could be established decisively, fixed for all time, by reference to objective, historical criteria. Henceforth, the text of Shakespeare was to be regarded, potentially, as monogenous, derived from a single source, rather than polygenous.

Malone's influence has proved decisive to the history of nineteenth- and twentieth-century bibliographic studies. Despite, however, the enormous growth in knowledge concerning the material processes of Elizabethan and Jacobean book production, the pursuit of Shakespeare's original words sanctioned a paradoxical distrust of precisely those early texts which Malone regarded as the touchstone of authenticity. Many assumed that these texts must themselves have been derived from some kind of authorial manuscript, and the possibility that Shakespeare's papers lay hidden somewhere exercised an insidious fascination upon the antiquarian imagination. Libraries were combed, lofts ransacked, and graves plundered, but the manuscripts have proved obstinately elusive, mute testimony to the low estimate an earlier culture had placed upon them once performance and publication had exhausted their commercial value.

Undeterred, scholars attempted to infer from the evidence of the early printed texts the nature of the manuscript which lay behind them. The fact that the various extant versions differed so consider- ably from each other posed a problem which could only be partially resolved by the designation of some as 'Bad Quartos', and therefore non-Shakespearean; for even the remaining 'authorised' texts varied between themselves enormously, invariably in terms of detail and often in terms of substance. Recourse to the concept of manuscript authenticity could not resolve the difficulty, for such a manuscript simply does not exist.[7] Faced with apparent textual anarchy, editors sought solace in Platonic idealism: each variant was deemed an imperfect copy of a perfect (if unobtainable) paradigm. Once again, the editor's task was to restore a lost original purity, employing compositor study, collation, conflation and emendation.[8]

Compositor study attempts to identify the working practices of the individuals who set the early quartos and the Folio, and thus differentiate the non-Shakespearean interference, stripping the 'veil of print from a text' and thus attempting 'to recover a number of precise details of the underlying manuscript.'[9] Collation, the critical comparison of different states of a text with a view to establishing the perfect condition of a particular copy, provided systematic classification of textual variations which could be regarded as putative corruptions. Emendation allows the editor to select one of the variations thrown up by collation and impose it upon the reading of the selected control text, or where no previous reading appeared satisfactory, to introduce a correction based upon editorial judgement. Conflation is employed to resolve the larger scale divergences between texts, so that, for example, the Folio *Hamlet* is often employed as the control text for modern editions of the play, but since it 'lacks' entire passages found only in the second quarto, these are often grafted on to the former to create the fullest 'authoritative' text.

The cuts to the Folio *Hamlet* may reflect, however, not a corruption introduced in the process of transmission, but a deliberate alteration to the text authorised by the dramatist himself. In recent years, the proposition that Shakespeare revised his work and that texts might therefore exist in a variety of forms has attracted considerable support. The most publicised debate has centred on the relationship of the quarto *History of King Lear* and the Folio *Tragedy of King Lear*.[10] The editors of the recent Oxford Shakespeare have broken new ground by including both texts in their one-volume edition on the grounds that the *Tragedy* represents an authorial revision of the earlier *History*, which is sufficiently radical to justify classifying it as a separate play. Wells and Taylor founded their revisionist position upon a recognition of the fact that

[5]

Shakespeare was primarily a working *dramatist* rather than literary author and that he addressed his play-texts towards a particular audience of theatrical professionals who were expected to flesh out the bare skeleton of the performance script: 'The written text of any such manuscript thus depended upon an unwritten para-text which always accompanied it: an invisible life-support system of stage directions, which Shakespeare could expect his first audience to supply, or which those first readers would expect Shakespeare himself to supply orally.'[11] They are thus more open than many of their predecessors to the possibility that texts reflect their theatrical provenance and therefore that a plurality of authorised texts may exist, at least for certain of the plays.[12] They remain, however, firmly author centred – the invisible life-support system can ultimately always be traced back to the dramatist himself and the plays remain under his parental authority.[13]

What, however, if it were not Shakespeare but the actor Burbage who suggested, or perhaps insisted on, the cuts to *Hamlet*? Would the Folio version of the play become unShakespearean? How would we react if we *knew* that the Clown spoke 'More than is set down' and that his ad libs were recorded? Or that the King's Men sanctioned additions by another dramatist for a Court performance? Or that a particular text recorded not the literary script of a play but its performance script? Of course, in one sense we cannot know these things. But drama, by its very nature, is overdetermined, the product of multiple influences simultaneously operating across a single site of cultural production. Eyewitness accounts of performances of the period suggest something of the provisionality of the scripts Shakespeare provided to his theatrical colleagues:

> After dinner on the 21st of september, at about two o'clock, I went with my companions over the water, and in the strewn roof-house saw the tragedy of the first Emperor Julius with at least fifteen characters very well acted. At the end of the comedy they danced according to their custom with extreme elegance. Two in men's clothes and two in women's gave this performance, in wonderful combination with each other.[14]

This passage offers what can seem a bizarre range of codes; the strewn roof-house, well-acted tragedy, comic aftermath and elegant

[6]

transvestite dance, hardly correspond to the typology of Shake-spearean drama our own culture has appropriated. The Swiss tourist Thomas Platter was in fact fortunate to catch the curious custom of the jig between Caesar and the boy dressed as Caesar's wife, for by 1612 'all Jigs, Rhymes and Dances' after plays had been 'utterly abolished' to prevent 'tumults and outrages whereby His Majesty's Peace is often broke'.[15] Shakespeare, however, is the 'author' of the spectacle Platter witnessed only in an extremely limited sense; in this context the dramatist's surname functions not simply to authenticate a literary masterpiece, but serves as a convenient if misleading shorthand term alluding to the complex material practices of the Elizabethan and Jacobean theatre industry.[16] It is in the latter sense that the term is used in this series.

Modern theoretical perspectives have destabilised the notion of the author as transcendant subject operating outside history and culture. This concept is in any event peculiarly inappropriate when applied to popular drama of the period. It is quite possible that, as Terence Hawkes argues, 'The notion of a single "authoritative" text, immediately expressive of the plenitude of its author's mind and meaning, would have been unfamiliar to Shakespeare, involved as he was in the collaborative enterprise of dramatic production and notoriously unconcerned to preserve in stable form the texts of most of his plays.'[17] The script is, of course, an integral element of drama, but it is by no means the only one. This is obvious in forms of representation, such as film, dependent on technologies which emphasise the role of the *auteur* at the expense of that of the writer. But even in the early modern theatre, dramatic realisation depended not just upon the scriptwriter,[18] but upon actors, entrepreneurs, promptbook keepers, audiences, patrons, etc; in fact, the entire wide range of professional and institutional interests constituting the theatre industry of the period.

Just as the scriptwriter cannot be privileged over all other influences, nor can any single script. It is becoming clear that within Elizabethan and Jacobean culture, around each 'Shakespeare' play there circulated a wide variety of texts, performing different theatrical functions and adopting different shapes in different contexts of production. Any of these contexts may be of interest to the modern reader. The so-called Bad Quartos, for example, are

General Introduction

generally marginalised as piratically published versions based upon the memorial reconstructions of the plays by bit-part actors. But even if the theory of memorial reconstruction is correct (and it is considerably more controversial than is generally recognised[19]), these quarto texts would provide a unique window on to the plays as they were originally performed and open up exciting opportunities for contemporary performance.[20] They form part, that is, of a rich diversity of textual variation which is shrouded by those traditional editorial practices which have sought to impose a single, 'ideal' paradigm.

In this series we have sought to build upon the pioneering work of Wells and Taylor, albeit along quite different lines. They argue, for example, that

> The lost manuscripts of Shakespeare's work are not the fiction of an idealist critic, but particular material objects which happen at a particular time to have existed, and at another particular time to have been lost, or to have ceased to exist. Emendation does not seek to construct an ideal text, but rather to restore certain features of a lost material object (that manuscript) by correcting certain apparent deficiencies in a second material object (this printed text) which purports to be a copy of the first. Most readers will find this procedure reasonable enough.[21]

The important emphasis here is on the relative status of the two forms, manuscript and printed text: the object of which we can have direct knowledge, the printed text, is judged to be corrupt by conjectural reference to the object of which we can by definition have no direct knowledge, the uncorrupted (but non-existent) manuscript. This corresponds to no philosophical materialism we have encountered. The editors of *Shakespearean Originals* reject the claim that it is possible to construct a rehabilitated text reflecting a form approximating Shakespeare's artistic vision.[22] Instead we prefer to embrace the early printed texts as authentic material objects, the concrete forms from which all subsequent editions ultimately derive.

We therefore present within this series particular textualisations of plays which are not necessarily canonical or indeed even written by *William Shakespeare, Gent*, in the traditional sense; but which nevertheless represent important facets of Shakespearean drama. In the same way that we have rejected the underlying principles of traditional editorial practice, we have also approached traditional editorial procedures with extreme caution, preferring to let the texts speak for themselves with a minimum of editorial mediation. We refuse to allow speculative judgements concerning the exact contribution of the various individuals involved in the production of a given text the authority to license alterations to that text, and as a result relegate compositor study and collation[23] to the textual apparatus rather than attempt to incorporate them into the text itself through emendation.

It seems to us that there is in fact no philosophical justification for emendation, which foregrounds the editor at the expense of the text. The distortions introduced by this process are all too readily incorporated into the text as holy writ. Macbeth's famous lines, for example, 'I dare do all that may become a man / Who dares do more is none,' on closer inspection turn out to be Rowe's. The Folio reads, 'I dare do all that may become a man / Who dares no more is none.' There seems to us no pressing reason whatsoever to alter these lines,[24] and we prefer to confine all such editorial speculation to the critical apparatus. The worst form of emendation is conflation. It is now widely recognised that the texts of the *The Historie of King Lear* (1608) and *The Tragedie of King Lear* (1623) differ so markedly that they must be considered as two distinct plays and that the composite *King Lear* which is reproduced in every twentieth-century popular edition of the play is a hybrid which grossly distorts both the originals from which it is derived. We believe that the case of *Lear* is a particularly clear example of a general proposition: that *whenever* distinct textualisations are conflated, the result is a hybrid without independent value. It should therefore go without saying that all the texts in this series are based upon single sources.

The most difficult editorial decisions we have had to face concern the modernisation of these texts. In some senses we have embarked upon a project of textual archaeology and the logic of our position points towards facsimile editions. These, however, are already available in specialist libraries, but they are there marginalised by those processes of cultural change which have rendered them alien and forbidding. Since we wish to challenge the hegemony of

General Introduction

standard editions by circulating the texts within this series as widely as possible, we have aimed at 'diplomatic' rather than facsimile status and have modernised those orthographic and printing conventions (such as long s, positional variants of u and v, i and j, ligatures and contractions) which are no longer current and likely to confuse. We do so, however, with some misgiving, recognising that as a result certain possibilities open to the Elizabethan reader are thereby foreclosed. On the other hand, we make no attempt to standardise such features as speech prefixes and *dramatis personae*, or impose conventions derived from naturalism, such as scene divisions and locations, upon the essentially fluid and non-naturalistic medium of the Elizabethan theatre. In order that our own editorial practice should be as open as possible we provide as an appendix a sample of the original text in photographic facsimile. The introductory essay attempts to view the play as a work of art in its own right rather than as an analogue to the received text, pointing towards those recent theoretical formulations which have validated its status and where possible to significant theatrical realisations. Annotation is kept deliberately light, but we do try to point out some of the performance possibilities occluded by traditional editorial mediations.

GRAHAM HOLDERNESS AND BRYAN LOUGHREY

NOTES AND REFERENCES

1. The title page of the popular *Titus Andronicus*, for example, merely records that it was 'Plaide by the Right Honourable the Earle of Darbie, Earle of Pembrooke, and Earle of Sussex their Servants', and not until 1598 was Shakespeare's name attached to a printed version of one of his plays, *Love's Labour's Lost*.
2. For a stimulating discussion of the relationship between the three texts of *Hamlet*, see Steven Urkowitz, '"Well-sayd olde Mole", Burying Three *Hamlets* in Modern Editions', in Georgianna Ziegler (ed.), *Shakespeare Study Today* (New York: AMS Press, 1986), pp. 37–70.
3. In the year of Shakespeare's death Ben Jonson staked a far higher claim for the status of the playwright, bringing out the first ever collected edition of English dramatic texts, *The Workes of Beniamin Jonson*, a carefully prepared and expensively produced folio volume. The text of his

General Introduction

Roman tragedy *Sejanus*, a play originally written with an unknown collaborator, was carefully revised to preserve the purity of authorial input. See Bryan Loughrey and Graham Holderness, 'Shakespearean Features', in Jean Marsden (ed.), *The Appropriation of Shakespeare: Post-Renaissance Reconstructions of the Works and the Myth* (Hemel Hempstead: Harvester Wheatsheaf, 1991), p. 183.

4. F. Madan and G.M.R. Turbutt (eds), *The Original Bodleian Copy of the First Folio of Shakespeare* (Oxford: Oxford University Press, 1905), p. 5.

5. Cited in D. Nicol Smith, *Eighteenth Century Essays* (Oxford: Oxford University Press, 1963), p. 48.

6. Margareta de Grazia, *Shakespeare Verbatim* (Oxford: Oxford University Press, 1991), p. 62. De Grazia provides the fullest and most stimulating account of the important theoretical issues raised by eighteenth-century editorial practice.

7. Unless the Hand D fragment of 'The Booke of Sir Thomas Moore' (British Library Harleian MS 7368) really is that of Shakespeare. See Stanley Wells and Gary Taylor, *William Shakespeare: A Textual Companion* (Oxford: Oxford University Press, 1987), pp. 461–7.

8. See Margaret de Grazia, 'The essential Shakespeare and the material book', *Textual Practice*, vol. 2, no. 1, spring 1988.

9. Fredson Bowers, 'Textual Criticism', in O.J. Campbell and E.G. Quinn (eds), *The Reader's Encyclopedia of Shakespeare* (New York: Methuen, 1966), p. 869.

10. See, for example, Gary Taylor and Michael Warren (eds), *The Division of the Kingdoms* (Oxford: Oxford University Press, 1983).

11. Stanley Wells and Gary Taylor, *William Shakespeare: A Textual Companion* (Oxford: Oxford University Press, 1987), p. 2.

12. See, for example, Stanley Wells 'Plural Shakespeare', *Critical Survey*, vol. 1, no. 1, spring 1989.

13. See, for example, *Textual Companion*, p. 69.

14. Thomas Platter, a Swiss physician who visited London in 1599 and recorded his playgoing; cited in *The Reader's Encyclopaedia*, p. 634. For a discussion of this passage see Richard Wilson, *Julius Caesar: A Critical Study* (Harmondsworth: Penguin, 1992), chapter 3.

15. E.K. Chambers, *The Elizabethan Stage* (Oxford: Oxford University Press, 1923), pp. 340–1.

16. The texts of the plays sometimes encode the kind of stage business Platter recorded. The epilogue of *2 Henry IV*, for example, is spoken by a dancer who announces that 'My tongue is weary; when my legs are too, I will bid you good night . . .'

17. Terence Hawkes, *That Shakespeherian Rag* (London, Methuen, 1986), p. 75.
18. For a discussion of Shakespeare's texts as dramatic scripts, see Jonathan Bate, 'Shakespeare's Tragedies as working scripts', *Critical Survey*, vol. 3, no. 2, 1991, pp. 118–27.
19. See, for example, Random Cloud [Randall McCleod], 'The Marriage of Good and Bad Quartos', *Shakespeare Quarterly*, vol. 33, no. 4, pp. 421–30.
20. See, for example, Bryan Loughrey, 'Q1 in modern performance', in Tom Clayton (ed.), *Q1 Now* (Minnesota, University of Nebraska Press, 1992) and Nicholas Shrimpton, 'Shakespeare Performances in London and Stratford-Upon-Avon, 1984–5', *Shakespeare Survey* 39, pp. 193–7.
21. *Textual Companion*, p. 60.
22. The concept of authorial intention, which has generated so much debate amongst critics, remains curiously unexamined within the field of textual studies.
23. Charlton Hinman's Norton Facsimile of *The First Folio of Shakespeare* offers a striking illustration of why this should be so. Hinman set out to reproduce the text of the original First Folio, but his collation of the Folger Library's numerous copies demonstrated that 'every copy of the finished book shows a mixture of early and late states of the text that is peculiar to it alone'. He therefore selected from the various editions those pages he believed represented the printer's final intentions and bound these together to produce something which 'has hitherto been only a theoretical entity, an abstraction: *the* First Folio'. Thus the technology which would have allowed him to produce a literal facsimile in fact is deployed to create an ahistorical composite which differs in substance from every single original upon which it is based. See Charlton Hinman, *The First Folio of Shakespeare* (New York, 1968), pp. xxiii–xxiv.
24. Once the process begins, it becomes impossible to adjudicate between rival conjectural emendations. In this case, for example, Hunter's suggestion that Lady Macbeth should be given the second of these lines seems to us neither more nor less persuasive than Rowe's.

Introduction

'Enormous dramatic economy and force' . . .
'a brisk, exciting play that lacks only the best qualities of subtlety
and poetry in the second, authentic quarto' . . .
'Great lines may be missing from this version but the vitality . . .
means that we never feel the loss' . . .
'the most entirely satisfactory piece of tragic acting of the year.'[1]

T H E S E phrases of positive celebration were ironically responses to
a performance (at the Orange Tree Theatre, Richmond, in 1985)
of a text then, as now, still routinely designated the 'Bad Quarto'
of Shakespeare's *Hamlet* – *The Tragicall Historie of Hamlet Prince of
Denmarke*, published in 1603. Though often still anxious to preserve
for this text, when compared to the other two Jacobean *Hamlet*
texts also ascribed to Shakespeare – *The Tragicall History of Hamlet
Prince of Denmarke* (1604), and *The Tragedie of Hamlet* (1623) – the
status of derivative or second rate, reviewers of that landmark 1985
production were none the less forcibly surprised by the theatrical
potentialities of the 'bad' text in performance. Since, however, it
is axiomatic, within the current diplomatic alliance of scholarship
and theatre studies, that dramatic texts receive their full realisation
only in performance, and that a text's performability must therefore
be considered an aspect of its literary quality, then the spectacle of
so much good springing out of badness presents a theoretical
problem of virtually theological dimensions.

It is generally conjectured that the First Quarto was pirated –
perhaps recorded and reconstructed from memory, possibly by one
of the actors who performed in it – and published without
permission of the author or his company. The Second Quarto
(some copies of which are dated 1604, some 1605), which bears on

[13]

Introduction

its title page the description 'Newly imprinted and enlarged to almost as much againe as it was, according to the true and perfect Coppie', would then have been a publication by dramatist and company of an authorised text. If that were the case, it would be reasonable to assume that the Second Quarto represents both Shakespeare's intended text and the version the company used for performances.

But this received account brings in its wake a host of problems. We do not know how the 1603 and 1604–5 texts found their way into print; but we do know that the same publisher, Nicholas Ling, printed both texts. We do not know what the Second Quarto claims to be a true and perfect copy of – the author's manuscript? the transcript prepared and submitted to the censor? the prompt-book? What we do know is that neither the Second Quarto nor the Folio texts (although the latter, an abridged and adapted version of Q2, bears many traces of playhouse influence) are likely to have represented acting versions: they are both, and especially Q2, inconveniently long. It would take some four hours to play the Second Quarto, even at high speed. In the nineteenth century, performances of the play were mounted using all the extant material from the two longer texts: known as 'the Entirity', this took six hours to play. Jacobean open-air performances took place approximately between two and four in the afternoon, the hours of optimum daylight; and of course the Chorus in *Romeo and Juliet* speaks of 'the two-hours traffic of our stage'. It is generally accepted that *The Tragicall Historie of Hamlet Prince of Denmarke* (1603) represents an acting version of the play. Whether it was a first, hastily prepared script, or a cut-down touring version; whether it was taken down from an actual performance, or hurriedly assembled from an uncompleted author's draft, it is scarcely possible to know with any certainty. What we can assume with reasonable confidence is that this text comes closer than the other texts to actual Jacobean stage practice.

Use of the term 'Bad Quarto' to identify a dramatic text supposedly reported or reconstructed from a theatrical performance permits a pervasive strategic dispersion of the attribution of 'badness', from a description of a particular mode of transmission (illegitimately copied from a performance rather than derived from some supposedly more authoritative source such as authorial manuscript, a scribal copy of the MS or an authorially 'approved' prompt-copy) to ascriptions of artistic or even moral 'badness' on the part of both the text and its conjectural producers. Just as ostensibly innocent bibliographical terms such as 'corruption' and 'contamination' carry far too strong a charge of ethical evaluation for their signifying power to operate purely at the level of objective scholarship,[2] so a 'Bad Quarto' can readily be received as not only bad in itself, but the product of bad men, the unscrupulous Elizabethan 'pirates', the ubiquitous 'playhouse thieves'.

The history of these 'Bad Quartos' in relation to performance goes right to the heart of the problem. The 'memorial reconstruction' theory holds that these texts are records of actual performances, though transcribed by an unreliable method, and printed without authorial approval. Even if the theory and its premises are accepted, the texts would remain uniquely valuable and interesting records of contemporary productions. As editorial policies have moved closer to the 'theatrical' text, one would have expected some revaluation of the 'Bad Quartos'; but this has simply not happened. Stanley Wells and Gary Taylor, who have done more than any other editors to validate the category of the theatrical text, remain disappointingly representative in their approach to the 'Bad Quartos'.[3] These texts exemplify, they assert, certain manifest faults, such as garbling, abbreviation, plagiarism, and 'cobbling'. They are 'post-performance texts' and therefore 'not without value in helping us to judge how Shakespeare's plays were originally performed'; but their usefulness is limited to the occasional preservation of an authentically Shakespearean contribution.

> Their stage directions may give us more information about how the plays were staged than is available in other texts: for instance, the reported text of *Hamlet* has the direction '*Enter Ofelia playing on a lute, and her hair down, singing*' – far more vivid than the good Quarto's '*Enter Ophelia*' or even the Folio's '*Enter Ophelia distracted*'. Because these are post-performance texts, they may preserve, in the midst of corruption, authentically Shakespearian changes made to the play after it was first written and not recorded elsewhere'.[4]

Despite the apocalyptic effect of the liturgical phrasing ('in the midst of corruption') all the term 'corruption' signifies here is some

level of intervention into the processes of composition and transmission by hands other than that of the author. Since we have no
means of knowing the extent to which authorial influence (as
distinct from the influences of actors, theatre entrepreneurs, scribes,
printers, pirates) uniquely determined the shape and content of the
printed texts, we are stuck with a self-evidently and irredeemably
collaborative cultural production. Why should this be a problem?
Since it is generally agreed that the early modern drama was a
highly collaborative cultural form, such collaboratively processed
scripts would seem accurate and appropriate products of its collective
methods. In practice, however, this general acceptance of the
'Shakespearean' drama as a collective rather than an individual
cultural form has not been permitted to dislodge the rigid hierarchy
of functions implicitly assumed by traditional editorial practices:
what the writer writes, others (actors, theatre entrepreneurs,
scribes, printers, pirates) corrupt, mangle and pervert to illegitimate
uses. The privileging and hypostatisation of the authorial function
is, of course, a retrospective anachronism; the pervasive assumption
of hierarchical precedence between the various functions (Shakespeare, for one, belonged to at least three of the categories listed
here) is an entirely inappropriate model of the historical conditions
of early modern culture.

If 'corruption', then, can be purged of its aura of moral trans-
gression and translated as the collaborative, overdetermined pro-
ductivity of the early modern theatre, in which the authentically
Shakespearian input happily coexisted with a diversity of other
influences, then Q1's validity as a performance-text can hardly be
questioned. Most of the so-called 'Bad Quartos' have, of course,
no post-Renaissance stage history, since they have never been
generally or accessibly available enough to be used in the theatre.
It is, however, abundantly clear that positive interest in these plays
as texts has depended on a recognition of their theatrical potentialities.
All we know of the original stage history of *The Tragicall Historie
of Hamlet Prince of Denmarke* (1603) is what the title page tells us,
that the play had 'been diverse times acted by his Highnesse
servants in the Cittie of London: as also in the two Universities of
Cambridge and Oxford, and elsewhere'. The play does, however,
have a subsequent performance history, of a minimal but sufficiently

Introduction

conclusive kind to invoke as evidence. The text was not rediscovered until 1823, in the form of an incomplete copy found by Sir Henry Bunbury (now in the Huntington Library, California); the copy now in the British Library came to light in 1856, when it was acquired by J.O. Halliwell, who sold it to the British Museum in 1858. It was republished, as a photolithographic facsimile, by William Griggs in 1880. Once published, it immediately caught the attention of William Poel, who wrote in the same year to F.J. Furnivall proposing a paper for the New Shakespeare Society on 'Acting Editions of Shakespeare'. Acknowledging that his comparison of the two Quarto texts had been enabled by the facsimile publications, Poel immediately recognised the 1603 version as a uniquely interesting performance-text:

> If to the literary student the Quarto of 1604 has the chief interest, I feel sure that to an actor the Quarto of 1603 has an equal interest, because . . . the actor cannot help recognising that the Editor has endeavoured to reproduce the play as *he* saw it represented and therefore in the arrangement of the scenes, the stage directions, the omissions, and the alterations, there is much to guide and instruct him in the stage representation of the play as it appeared in Shakespeare's time. There was so much that was new and interesting to me, from a dramatic point of view, in the first Quarto, that I could not help thinking, if the printer's blunders could be corrected, a performance of the Quarto might be of some interest to students . . .⁵

The Tragicall Historie of Hamlet Prince of Denmarke (1603) received a virtually amateur performance (with Poel playing Hamlet) on 16 April 1881. The production was conceived in spare and minimalist terms: though making extensive use of curtains and lighting effects, Poel aimed at the visual austerity of the Globe stage (a stage-plan in the prompt-book positions a bench exactly where the same object stands in de Witt's drawing of the Swan theatre). Q1's stage directions were followed to the letter: some amusement was caused among the audience by the Ghost entering 'in his night gowne' (see p. 81). The most elaborate staging design called for by the text, the 'play-within-a-play' scene, was arranged simply on the virtually bare stage, with four chairs and a stool facing a low wooden platform. Unfavourable reviews criticised the production for its austerity – 'conditions which rendered success more than an

Introduction

improbability'[6] – and its amateur acting. Their primary target was however, predictably, the text: a 'degraded text', a 'muddled and mangled text', a 'corrupt play'; 'the rough sketch of a play . . . a mutilated *Hamlet*; 'the "botcher's text", the barbarously mutilated and imperfect version of the piratical printer'.[7]

Poel, initially, as is clear from the above quotation, regarded Q1 as a pirated memorial reconstruction, theatrically interesting precisely in proportion to its performance origin. After the St George's Hall production he seems to have shifted (perhaps persuaded, Marion O'Connor suggests, by Furnivall[8]) towards the revisionist theory of Q1 as an early authorial draft. Poel's own version of the revision theory is, however, interestingly idiosyncratic, since it proposes a model of contradictory development in which revision towards literary perfection can simultaneously be seen as revision away from theatrical effectiveness. Q2 may represent the play 'as it finally left Shakespeare's hand'; but the developmental process of the text may have been in some senses a retrograde one:

> I . . . contend that, as Shakespeare himself must have been aware of the acting value which the play had lost by its development into literary perfection, Quarto I represents more truly his dramatic conception than either Quarto II or our stage version. Accepting Quarto I as Shakespeare's first draft of the play (though clumsily pirated as to language) I think one ought to arrange a stage version from the authentic text upon the lines laid down in Quarto I rather than sacrifice dramatic coherence for the sake of bringing in all the beautiful passages.[9]

This adroit attempt to negotiate the contradictory pressures of scholarly evaluation and theatrical potentiality establishes a theoretical configuration within which *The Tragicall Historie of Hamlet Prince of Denmarke* (1603) continues to be received and addressed.

William Poel's production subsequently interested Sam Walters, Artistic Director of the Orange Tree Theatre, Richmond, when he read of it while directing at the Webber Douglas Drama School. The text was performed there by students, and later given a professional production, directed by Sam Walters, in 1985 at the Orange Tree. Reviewing the latter production in *Shakespeare Survey*, Nicholas Shrimpton celebrated the performance as 'the most entirely satisfactory piece of tragic acting of the year'.[10] As suggested earlier, this positive response to the text in performance does not produce any revaluation of the text itself. On the contrary, Shrimpton manages to hold the traditional negative evaluation of the text as 'Bad Quarto', together with his fulsome acknowledgement of its unquestionable theatrical quality.

> The text itself, for all its imperfections, contributed something to the freshness of the playing . . . Even the oddity had its advantages. Listening to the First Quarto in performance proved to be an experience not unlike hearing the New English Bible read in church. It is commonplace but clear . . . 'To be or not to be, I there's the point' commanded an intense attention which I have rarely seen the uncorrupted text achieve in the theatre . . . First Quarto is a lesser text than its alternatives. But this production gave clarity, energy and tension to the ideas which it does contain . . .[11]

That so much freshness, clarity, intensity, energy and tension should be produced from a lesser, imperfect, corrupt, odd, commonplace text suggests some remarkable complexity in the relations between text and performance. The contradictory pattern of Shrimpton's response (a bad text, but a rattling good evening's entertainment) can be found embedded as a deep structure in earlier press reviews of the Orange Tree performance: 'Never mind lines like "To be, or not to be, I there's the point" . . . the 1603 edition of *Hamlet* is a brisk, exciting play that lacks only the best qualities of subtlety and poetry in the second, authentic quarto.' 'Great lines may be missing from this version but the vitality . . . means that we never feel the loss.' Other reviewers refer to 'the First Quarto of *Hamlet*, a "bad" pirated text which, although verbally garbled, nevertheless has enormous dramatic economy and force'; or describe how 'the rarely performed first quarto (probably pirated, probably based on faulty memory) skims through the classic text with quite disconcerting results'.[12] Is it not possible, on the contrary, that the qualities produced in performance are authentic potentialities of the text, arising not from the 'fortuitous oddity' of its intertextual invocation of the 'good' texts, and not only from the mediation of conditions of production: but from the text's own intrinsic theatrical capacities?

A brief trawl through some of the standard modern editions indicates how readily *The Tragicall Historie of Hamlet Prince of*

Introduction

Denmarke (1603) is constituted, once the hypothesis of memorial reconstruction is established (at least to editorial satisfaction), as a mere whipping boy to the putatively 'good' texts, Q2 and F. Harold Jenkins in the Arden edition accepted G.I. Duthie's view of Q1 as a 'bad quarto', and was hence able to explain 'the various corruptions of Q1 – omissions, mislinings, paraphrases, verbal and morphological substitutions, misunderstandings, transpositions, anticipations and recollections' as 'the recognized signs of a play reconstructed from memory'.[13] G.R. Hibbard (Oxford Shakespeare) is even more forthright in his condemnation of the text: 'Duthie showed, beyond all reasonable doubt, that the quarto of 1603 is a reported text . . . Q1 is, as it stands, a sorry thing, and, from the editor's point of view, an extremely unreliable one'.[14] Philip Edwards (New Cambridge Shakespeare) concurs: 'The first quarto is a much-abbreviated as well as a much-debased version of Shakespeare's play . . . There is little dispute that the first quarto is a "reported" text, an attempt to put together the text of a play from memory without recourse or access to an authoritative manuscript'.[15]

Once it becomes generally accepted that *The Tragicall Historie of Hamlet Prince of Denmarke* (1603) should be regarded as a memorial reconstruction of an original performance, a text which has by-passed the crucial relationship to an authorial manuscript, the scholarly obligation becomes a simple task of invidious comparison, calculated to establish the superiority and originality of the other two texts, and requiring the release of tirades of rhetorical invective against the pirate or pirates responsible for the production of the 'Bad Quarto'. 'The unauthorised nature of this quarto' writes Harold Jenkins 'is matched by the corruptness of its text' (Arden, p. 14). Waving aside objections from those who observe that there is no evidence of any such practice as 'memorial reconstruction', Jenkins indicates that the 'corruption' involved is tantamount to homicide: 'if you come upon a mutilated corpse you don't deny a murder because nobody has reported one' (Arden, p. 20). Hibbard writes of Q1 as filled with 'passages of sheer nonsense' (Oxford, p. 69), 'bad grammar and senseless punctuation' (Oxford, p. 70), 'badly mangled relics of their counterparts, full of synonyms, halting in metre, shaky in grammar, and deficient in sense'

[20]

(Oxford, p. 72). The pirate responsible is stigmatised, as is customary in these cases, for stupidity: 'The reporter could not reconstruct the speech because he had never properly understood it. A failure to comprehend compounds the errors due to a failure to remember' (Oxford, p. 85). For Philip Edwards, the badness of the text is so self-evident as to require no demonstration: Q1's version of the 'To be or not to be' soliloquy is a 'standard example of its quality' (New Cambridge, p. 24). Even the putative link with performance carries no promise of redemption, since 'the nearer we get to the stage the further we are getting from Shakespeare' (New Cambridge, p. 32). More often a grudging concession is made to the potential usefulness of the text in terms of its relation to a history of performance; though there is never any suggestion that such a theatrical relationship might call for a revaluation of the dramatic text. 'The usefulness of Q1 is . . . that it throws light on the theatrical and textual history of the play' (Jenkins, Arden, p. 36). 'Its main value, however, lies in this: that through the fog, growing thicker as the play goes on and recollection becomes fainter, one catches glimpses of an acting version of the tragedy current in the early seventeenth century' (Hibbard, Oxford, p. 89). 'The one link we have with *Hamlet* as acted at the Globe theatre is the first quarto of 1603' (Edwards, New Cambridge, p. 24).

It will be observed that all these imputed characteristics of the 'bad' text depend on its relation to the 'good' texts: our guide to the badness of the one is the demonstrable goodness of the others. In fact many of the detailed comparisons originally offered by Duthie and subsequently represented for endorsement by *Hamlet*'s editors, will withstand very little serious examination once the Quarto text is addressed as an appropriate object of investigation in its own right. Particular observations alleging inconsistency of plot or motive, or apparent contradictions in character or audience knowledge of events, can be made against virtually any Elizabethan dramatic text. Such objections depend on anachronistic conceptions of time and space, and quickly recede in importance when the play is presented (as it is in this edition) without the act and scene divisions subsequently added by editorial interference. Detailed stylistic comparisons can seem equally unconvincing. Harold Jenkins argues that Q1 for example often prints 'the right words in the wrong order' (Arden, p. 23). The example he gives is Q1's 'so gracious and so hallow'd', where Q2 has 'so hallow'd and so gracious'. Jenkins knows these are the right words, as they are in Q2; and he is further confident that they appear in that text 'in the right order'. But how does he know which is the right order?

Frequently, such local comparison of variant readings bring into play assumptions about poetic language which seem highly question-able when more closely inspected. Jenkins writes for example of the 'absurdity of the sepulchre which has *burst* [Q1], instead of *oped* [actually 'op't', Q2, or 'op'd', F] its marble jaws'. But is not the specific critical judgement made there more than questionable? Could we not prefer to the smoothly sliding automatic doors of Q2 the metaphysical extremity of verbal violence in the '*burst*' of Q1? Shouldn't it hurt for a ghost to leave the tomb?[16] When memory fails, the pirate characteristically parrots 'bits of other plays' to pad out the consequent lacunae. The parrot–pirate of Q1, for example, found, Jenkins asserts (Arden, p. 30), a convenient tag-line from *Twelfth Night* ('we men . . . prove / Much in our vows, but little in our love') and adapted it for Corambis to round off a scene: 'such men often prove, / Great in their wordes, but little in their love'. When we examine the context in Q1 (see below, p. 48) we find, however, that Corambis's use of the couplet is actually bracketed, like many of his wise saws and modern instances, in quotation marks, a device by means of which this text uniquely distinguishes the old bore's formal quotations from more direct speech. Presumably he quotes the same well-known jingle from which Viola's line was derived, though there it is not, of course, marked as quotation. Perhaps we should be considering the possibility of plagiarism in relation to *Twelfth Night* (a Bad Folio?) rather than Q1.

To enter into a detailed defence of *The Tragicall Historie of Hamlet Prince of Denmarke* (1603) against this tradition of comparative condemnation cannot be done without complicity in the established parameters of this bibliographical problematic – piracy, memorial reconstruction, the self–evident inferiority of a 'stolne, and surrep-titious cop[y]'. In a hierarchical configuration of texts separated by principles of moral discrimination, priority is automatically given to the readings of the texts adjudged 'good'. On a level playing-

Introduction

field of textual plurality, variant readings can be objectively compared and apprehended as different from one another, without any establishing of discursive hierarchy. As Stephen Urkowitz has pointed out, the 'memorial reconstruction' hypothesis itself

> seems to have prevented close examination of the fundamental documents of our literary–dramatic tradition by its practitioners, teachers of literature and performers of plays. Labeling certain texts as 'bad' quartos has removed them from the normal discourse in which such documents would otherwise be included.[17]

Although Urkowitz leans, like Stanley Wells and Gary Taylor, towards a view of the multiple texts as indications of authorial revision – thus clinging to an umbilical cord firmly attaching the texts to an 'author' – his key emphasis is surely correct: the various surviving printed texts of early modern drama should be accepted as the 'fundamental documents', and should be 'studied for what they are, in and of themselves, rather than solely as pernicious desecrations of Shakespeare's iconic originals'.[18]

We have indicated that in critical responses to the play in performance there is a clear recurrent pattern of divergence and opposition between textual and theatrical evaluations. In the testimony of theatre practitioners who, like William Poel, have been involved in producing *The Tragicall Historie of Hamlet Prince of Denmarke* (1603), this contradiction deepens and intensifies to a point where those aspects that scholars and critics regard as the shortcomings of the text reappear in the context of theatre practice as positive creative possibilities. The abbreviation of the text (Q1 consists of some 2,200 lines compared with Q2's 3,800) is generally considered only in terms of loss. But if Q1 is addressed, as it was initially received by its first Jacobean spectators, as a play in its own right, then what we find is not a reduced and diminished version of Q2, but a different and particular dramatic shape which happens to offer a tighter dramatic narrative and a faster theatrical denouement. Variations of action, character, language between *The Tragicall Historie of Hamlet Prince of Denmarke* (1603) and the other two texts are invariably thought of in terms of theoretical models of defect and norm, aberration and ideal, periphery and centre. If we replace these models, with their impossible aspiration towards the unrealis-

[23]

Introduction

able ideal of a single perfect text, with an alternative problematic of textual plurality and discursive multiplicity, then the availability of a text sufficiently different to be accepted as alternative can only be welcomed. Christopher McCullough, who played the role of Hamlet in a university production of Q1, suggests that the existence of such an alternative textualisation effectively destabilises the traditional notion of authorial integrity and completeness.[19]

McCullough had an opportunity of discussing his experience of *The Tragicall Historie of Hamlet Prince of Denmarke* (1603), together with Sam Walters, who directed it at the Orange Tree, and Peter Gillis, who played the title role in that production, in an interview conducted in 1990. Point for point, the views of actors and director as to the theatrical quality of the text directly contradict the scholarly and critical consensus of its literary value. The abbreviated nature of the text produced an accelerated dramatic narrative that rendered the play more accessible, and also inflected it significantly away from some of the traditional assumptions that derive from familiarity with the received, conflated text. Peter Gillis found the text of Q1 resisting the conventional interiorisation of action within the tragic subject: the problems of the play became less psychological, more circumstantial and contingent:

> Playing as we did in the little room over the Orange Tree pub theatre, I can remember very clearly that as I stepped onto the acting area, Hamlet was on his way to take revenge on Claudius; and in the time it took to cross those few feet that make up the Orange Tree acting area, to the room next door which was where Claudius was at his prayers, Hamlet merely pauses for thought, for a moment's soul-searching – and he is then interrupted by Ophelia, I played that speech with the dagger in my hand: 'To be or not to be' – the dagger was in my hand, my sleeves were rolled up as it were, Hamlet was on his way to do the job. And simply in walking down the corridor to Claudius's room, he voices thoughts that momentarily impede his progress towards that room: and then he's side-tracked by Ophelia. But at the top of that speech he's on his way to do it . . . Had he not been interrupted, he'd have just taken a beat or two, his hand would have gone onto the door handle, the door would have opened, there would have been Claudius – and bang, he'd have done it, there and then.[20]

[24]

Introduction

Christopher McCullough recalled the accelerated narrative producing a particular emphasis on the political rather than the psychological dimension:

> For us, the speed of the narrative opened up the politics of the play. Because there was less time spent on introspection and on the character of Hamlet, the attention of both actors and audience was directed much more towards the political setup dramatised in the play . . . The killing of Claudius didn't become the sole focus: it was part of something much bigger, a historical interplay between the older feudal world of Hamlet senior, and the modern political world of this new Renaissance despot, Claudius.[21]

The 'Bad Quarto' hypothesis would, of course, explain these responses as symptomatic of the text's relative crudity, since it appears to invest significance in action and exterior event rather than in a psychological landscape of character: it is a drama of action, a melodrama perhaps, rather than a drama of passionate consciousness, a great poetic tragedy. But the witness of the theatre practitioners proposes that experiential complexity was transferred rather than lost, shifted from the self-conscious subject to a dialectical relationship between actor and audience. The soliloquies, McCullough suggests, seem to have been written not as the stuff of brooding introspection, but as the raw material of an active exchange between character and audience:

> I think the way the soliloquies are handled in Q1 provides very important clues to Elizabethan theatre practice. The general understanding of the Shakespearean soliloquy is a very post-Romantic notion, of something very introspective. We think of Redgrave and Gielgud and Olivier – Olivier in his film actually disembodied his soliloquies into voice-overs: and that perhaps is as far as you can go in the direction of introspection. But those lines, 'To be or not to be, I there's the point' perhaps give us a clue as to how the soliloquies were worked, how that particular convention was used in the Elizabethan theatre.
>
> In my own experience of playing the text I couldn't perform 'I there's the point' by turning in on myself and pretending there wasn't an audience there. 'To be or not to be, – I there's the *point*' actually only made sense if I said it *to the audience*. In fact I was using the soliloquy as a way of putting an argument to the audience as to

what was going on in the narrative: and I think in that sense the First Quarto is giving us clues about the much more open-ended nature of Elizabethan theatre.[22]

Peter Gillis found Q1's alternative version of the familiar soliloquy – contemptuously dismissed by Philip Edwards as 'standard example of its quality' (New Cambridge, p. 24) – both artistically superior and productive of interestingly divergent audience responses:

> The audience is suddenly presented with 'To be or not to be, I there's the point'. Some nights, of course, depending on the composition of our audience, that would produce a huge, cynical, knowing laugh, the reaction of those who were confident they know the right words. On other occasions, the audience reaction would be one of genuine but delighted surprise: 'To be or not to be, I there's the point' didn't produce a smirk, but rather a smile of delight, because somehow it's a much more muscular line to deliver, and has much more of an impact than the 'traditional' form of words . . . in keeping with the whole of the First Quarto it has an energy and an edge that the Folio in all its refinement, particularly its poetic refinement, doesn't have.[23]

As far as scholars and editors are concerned, the versions of Hamlet's soliloquies to be found in *The Tragicall Historie of Hamlet Prince of Denmarke* (1603) are representative of its failure to approximate to their notion of true original copy. Here, at those points traditionally regarded as the heights of poetic complexity and psychological truth, the pirate's intellectual qualifications render him sadly incompetent even to understand, let alone correctly reproduce, what he has heard. Quoting Q1's soliloquy 'O that this too much griev'd and sallied flesh' (see below, p. 43), G.R. Hibbard conjecturally describes the flounderings of a dumb incompetent:

> Some phrases, and even some lines, stick in his head; but he has no idea of the order in which they occur or of the way in which they are related to one another. The outcome of his effort to recall what he heard is, to use his own words, 'a Chaos' . . . muddle is written all over it. The reporter could not reconstruct the speech because he had never properly understood it.[24]

Peter Gillis describes his own experience of acting the same soliloquy from a very different perspective:

this particular version of the play came across to me, once I started to work on it, in a very immediate sense: it is unrefined, it hasn't been tidied up (as perhaps the Folio has been tidied up), and for an actor, a play that falls on occasions into that rather stumbling language can provide a great challenge, and indeed a gift, because a lot of the thinking that one has to invent when one is working with a crafted script, doesn't come into the playing of the First Quarto: all those stumbling thoughts, those half-thoughts, those unfinished sentences, those uncompleted ideas, are actually there: it really is a *working* text.[25]

All three of the theatre practitioners involved in this discussion concurred, often from different points of observation, in this concept of *The Tragicall Historie of Hamlet Prince of Denmarke* (1603) as a 'working text', both in the sense of its historical origins and of its continuing theatrical potentiality. McCullough proposed that in that sense this text is more valuable to actors and directors than the two texts traditionally accepted and appropriated as 'literary' masterpieces:

what the First Quarto is pointing us towards, with that stumbling of the dialogue . . . is not literature, but theater practice. The First Quarto speaks to us of what might have been happening on the Jacobean stage . . . it is pointing us much more towards contemporary theatrical practice, and towards what the original Shakespearean *Hamlet* in performance may have been about. There are all sorts of clues in the play about how actors were working; and that is really what's exciting for me, that we're seeing the possibilities of theatrical energy, of the way space was used, of how actors related to audiences.[26]

Thus the 'working text' used by Jacobean actors to produce the *Hamlet* of the early seventeenth century is of both historical and contemporary interest and value. This edition now makes the play generally available, for the first time since the early seventeenth century, for the kind of practical experimentation and theoretical mobilisation which alone can genuinely test the validity of that scholarly consensus that has kept this play now, for the best part of two centuries, on the margins of editorial reproduction, critical debate and theatrical performance.

Introduction

NOTES AND REFERENCES

1. The quotations are taken respectively from the following sources:
   Andrew Rissick, *Time Out*, 14 March 1985; B.A. Young, *Financial Times*, 5 March 1985; Desmond Christy, *The Guardian*, April 1985; Nicholas Shrimpton, *Shakespeare Survey*, 39 (1987), p. 197.

2. Randall McCleod ironically suggests that neutral terms such as 'gad' and 'bood' should be substituted for 'good' and 'bad', precisely to avoid the elision of bibliographical categories and moral judgements: see Random Cloud [Randall McCleod], 'The Marriage of Good and Bad Quartos', *Shakespeare Quarterly* 33:4 (1982), pp. 421–30.

3. Stanley Wells and Gary Taylor (eds), *William Shakespeare: the complete works* (Oxford: Oxford University Press, 1986), pp. xxx–xxxiii.

4. *Ibid.*, p. xxxi.

5. Letter of William Poel to F.J. Furnivall (1 February 1881), quoted in Marion O'Connor, *William Poel and the Elizabethan Stage Society* (London: Chadwick-Healey/Consortium for Drama and Media in Higher Education, 1987), p. 21.

6. *The Morning Post*, 18 April 1881; quoted in O'Connor (1987), pp. 20 and 116n.

7. *The Saturday Review*. 23 April 1881, p. 526; Dutton Cook, 'The *Hamlet* of 1603', in *Nights at the Play* (London: Chatto & Windus, 1883), pp. 454–5; *The Morning Post*, 18 April 1881, p. 7; *The Era*, 23 April 1881, p. 4. Quoted in O'Connor (1987), pp. 21 and 116n.

8. See O'Connor (1987), p. 21.

9. Letter of William Poel to *The Era*, published 23 April 1881, p. 4. Quoted in O'Connor (1987), p. 22 and p. 116n.

10. Shrimpton (1987), pp. 194–7.

11. *Ibid.*

12. Young (1985), Christy (1985), Rissick (1985) – as in note 1; and Christine Eccles, *City Limits*, 8 March 1985.

13. Harold Jenkins (ed.), *The Arden Shakespeare: Hamlet* (London: Methuen, 1982), pp. 18–36; G.I. Duthie, *The 'Bad' Quarto of 'Hamlet'* (Cambridge: Cambridge University Press, 1941), p. 19.

14. G.R. Hibbard (ed.) *The Oxford Shakespeare: Hamlet* (Oxford: Clarendon Press, 1987), p. 89.

15. Philip Edwards (ed.) *The New Cambridge Shakespeare: Hamlet* (Cambridge: Cambridge University Press, 1985), p. 25.

16. Nicholas Shrimpton imagines that this 'bad' reading was replaced in the Orange Tree production by the 'good' form of words: 'Walters had, reasonably enough, made absolute fidelity subordinate to the needs of performance and tidied up a few of the more ludicrous or

confusing variants. King Hamlet's sepulchre, accordingly, "op'd" rather than burst his ponderous and marble jaws' (p. 195). We, on the contrary, heard the sepulchre 'burst'; and Sam Walters confirms that they made no alterations of this kind to the text: 'We did it in a rather purist way, and didn't as it were "correct" the text' – see Bryan Loughrey, 'Q1 in recent performance: an interview', in Thomas Clayton (ed.), *Q1 Now* (Minnesota: University of Nebraska Press, 1991), pp. 123–36.

17. Stephen Urkowitz, 'Good news about bad quartos', in Maurice Charney (ed.), *Bad Shakespeare: revaluations of the Shakespeare canon* (London and Toronto: Associated University Presses, 1988), p. 204.
18. *Ibid.*, p. 204.
19. Loughrey, 'Q1 in recent performance', p. 128.
20. *Ibid.*, pp. 130–1.
21. *Ibid.*, p. 131.
22. *Ibid.*, p. 126.
23. *Ibid.*, p. 125.
24. Hibbard, *The Oxford Shakespeare: Hamlet*, pp. 84–5.
25. Loughrey, 'Q1 in recent performance', p. 124.
26. *Ibid.*, pp. 124–5.

Select Bibliography

Bate, Jonathan, 'Shakespeare's tragedies as working scripts', *Critical Survey*, 3:ii (1991), pp. 118–27.

Clayton, Thomas, (ed.), *Q1 Now* (Minnesota: University of Nebraska Press, 1991).

Cloud, Random [Randall McCleod], 'The marriage of good and bad quartos', *Shakespeare Quarterly* 33:4 (1982), pp. 421–30.

Duthie, G.I., *The 'Bad' Quarto of 'Hamlet'* (Cambridge: Cambridge University Press, 1941).

Edwards, Philip (ed.) *The New Cambridge Shakespeare: Hamlet* (Cambridge: Cambridge University Press, 1985).

Furness, Horace Howard (ed.) *Hamlet: a new variorum edition* (1877) (New York: Dover Publications, 1963), vol. 2.

Grazia, Margareta de, 'The Essential Shakespeare and the material book', *Textual Practice*, 2:i (1988), pp. 69–85.

Grazia, Margareta de, *Shakespeare Verbatim* (Oxford: Oxford University Press, 1991).

Hibbard, G.R. (ed.) *The Oxford Shakespeare: Hamlet* (Oxford: Clarendon Press, 1987).

Holderness, Graham, *Hamlet* (Milton Keynes: Open University Press, 1987).

Ioppolo, Grace, *Revising Shakespeare* (Cambridge, Mass.: Harvard University Press, 1991).

Jenkins, Harold (ed.), *The Arden Shakespeare: Hamlet* (London: Methuen, 1982).

Marcus, Leah, 'Levelling Shakespeare: local customs and local texts', *Shakespeare Quarterly*, 42:ii (1991), pp. 168–78.

Loughrey, Bryan, 'Q1 in recent performance: an interview', in Clayton, Thomas (ed.), *Q1 Now* (Minnesota: University of Nebraska Press, 1991).

O'Connor, Marion, *William Poel and the Elizabethan Stage Society* (London:

Select Bibliography

Chadwick-Healey/Consortium for Drama and Media in Higher Education, 1987).

Orgel, Stephen, 'The authentic Shakespeare', *Representations* 21 (winter 1988), pp. 1–26.

Parker, Brian, 'Bowers of bliss: deconflation in the Shakespeare canon', *New Theatre Quarterly*, 7: xxv (1991), pp. 357–61.

Shrimpton, Nicholas, 'Shakespeare performances in London and Stratford-upon-Avon, 1984–5', *Shakespeare Survey 39* (1987), pp. 193–7.

Small, Ian and Marcus Walsh (eds), *The Theory and Practice of Text-editing* (Cambridge: Cambridge University Press, 1991).

Urkowitz, Stephen, '"Well-sayd olde Mole": burying three *Hamlets* in modern editions', in Georgianna Zeigler (ed.), *Shakespeare Study Today* (New York: Ams Press, 1986), pp. 37–70.

Urkowitz, Stephen, 'Good News about Bad Quartos', in Maurice Charney (ed.), *Bad Shakespeare: Revaluations of the Shakespeare Canon* (London and Toronto: Associated University Presses, 1988).

Wells, Stanley, 'Theatricalizing Shakespeare's texts', *New Theatre Quarterly*, 7:xxvi (1991), pp. 184–6.

Wells, Stanley and Gary Taylor (eds), *William Shakespeare: the complete works*, and *William Shakespeare: the complete works, original-spelling edition* (Oxford: Oxford University Press, 1986).

Wells, Stanley and Gary Taylor, *William Shakespeare: A textual companion* (Oxford: Oxford University Press, 1987).

Textual History

T H E Tragicall Historie of Hamlet Prince of Denmarke was published in
1603, under the following title-page inscription:

> The
> Tragicall Historie of
> HAMLET
> Prince of Denmarke
> By William Shake-speare

> As it hath beene diverse times acted by his Highnesse
> servants in the Cittie of London: as also in the two
> Universities of Cambridge and Oxford, and elsewhere

> At London printed for N[icholas] L[ing] and Iohn Trundell.
> 1603.

I T was the first surviving text of any *Hamlet* play to be printed. The
text was not rediscovered until 1823, in the form of an incomplete
copy found by Sir Henry Bunbury, who believed the text had been
collected by his grandfather Sir William Bunbury. Sir Henry
discovered it loosely bound up with several other Shakespeare
quartos, and sold it to a bookseller who then sold it on to the Duke
of Devonshire. This text is now in the Huntington Library,
California. The complete copy (lacking only the title-page) now in
the British Library (on which this edition is based) came to light
in 1856, when a Dublin bookseller bought it from a student of
Trinity College. He afterwards disposed of it to J.O. Halliwell,
who sold it to the British Museum in 1858. The Huntington copy

was published in facsimile in 1858, and reprinted as a parallel text with the 1604 quarto in 1860. The British Library copy was reprinted as a photolithographic facsimile, by William Griggs, in 1880.

The text has been published in original-spelling form by Horace Howard Furness in the *New Variorum Edition of Shakespeare: Hamlet* (London: J.B. Lippincott, 1877; reprinted New York: Dover Publications, 1963), vol 2; Geoffrey Bullough, *Narrative and Dramatic Sources of Shakespeare*, vol. 7 (London: Routledge and Kegan Paul, 1973); and Michael Allen and Kenneth Muir (eds), *Shakespeare's Plays in Quarto* (Berkeley and Los Angeles: California University Press, 1981). Photographic facsimiles have been published, one with a critical apparatus by W.W. Greg (Oxford: Clarendon Press, 1940), and another in *Hamlet: First Quarto, 1603* (Menston: Scolar Press, 1969).

THE
Tragicall Historie of
HAMLET
Prince of Denmarke

By William Shake-speare.

As it hath beene diuerse times acted by his Highnesse ser-
uants in the Cittie of London : as also in the two V-
niuersities of Cambridge and Oxford, and else-where

At London printed for N.L. and Iohn Trundell.
1603.

Hamlet
Prince of Denmarke

Enter two Centinels.

1. Stand: who is that?
2. Tis I.
1. O you come most carefully upon your watch,
2. And if you meete *Marcellus* and *Horatio*,
The partners of my watch, bid them make haste.
1. I will : See who goes there.

Enter Horatio and Marcellus.

Hor. Friends to this ground.
Mar. And leegemen to the Dane,
O farewell honest souldier, who hath releeved you?
1. Barnardo hath my place, give you good night.
Mar. Holla, *Barnardo*.
2. Say, is *Horatio* there?
Hor. A peece of him.
2. Welcome *Horatio*, welcome good *Marcellus*.
Mar. What hath this thing appear'd againe to night.
2. I have seene nothing.
Mar. Horatio sayes tis but our fantasie,
And wil not let beliefe take hold of him,
Touching this dreaded sight twice seene by us,
Therefore I have intreated him along with us

To watch the minutes of this night,
That if againe this apparition come,
He may approove our eyes, and speake to it.

   Hor. Tut, t'will not appeare.

   2. Sit downe I pray, and let us once againe
Assaile your eares that are so fortified,
What we have two nights seene.

   Hor. Wel, sit we downe, and let us heare *Bernardo* speake
of this.

   2. Last night of al, when yonder starre that's west-
ward from the pole, had made his course to
Illumine that part of heaven. Where now it burnes,
The bell then towling one.

               Enter Ghost.

   Mar. Breake off your talke, see where it comes againe.

   2. In the same figure like the King that's dead,

   Mar. Thou art a scholler, speake to it *Horatio.*

   2. Lookes it not like the king?

   Hor. Most like, it horrors mee with feare and wonder.

   2. It would be spoke to.

   Mar. Question it *Horatio.*

   Hor. What art thou that thus usurps the state, in
Which the Majestie of buried *Denmarke* did sometimes
Walke? By heaven I charge thee speake.

   Mar. It is offended.   *exit Ghost.*

   2. See, it stalkes away.

   Hor. Stay, speake, speake, by heaven I charge thee
speake.

   Mar. Tis gone and makes no answer.

   2. How now *Horatio*, you tremble and looke pale,
Is not this something more than fantasie?
What thinke you on't?

   Hor. Afore my God, I might not this beleeve, without
the sensible and true avouch of my owne eyes.

   Mar. Is it not like the King?

Hor. As thou art to thy selfe,
Such was the very armor he had on,
When he the ambitious *Norway* combated.
So frownd he once, when in an angry parle
He smot the sleaded pollax on the yce,
Tis strange.
    Mar. Thus twice before, and jump at this dead hower,
With Marshall stalke he passed through our watch.
    Hor. In what particular to worke, I knowe not,
But in the thought and scope of my opinion,
This bodes some strange eruption to the state.
    Mar. Good, now sit downe, and tell me he that knowes
Why this same strikt and most observant watch,
So nightly toyles the subject of the land,
And why such dayly cost of brazen Cannon
And forraine marte, for implements of warre,
Why such impresse of ship-writes, whose sore taske
Does not divide the sunday from the weeke:
What might be toward that his sweaty march
Doth make the night joynt labourer with the day,
Who is't that can informe me?
    Hor. Mary that can I, at least the whisper goes so,
Our late King who as you know was by Forten-
Brasse of *Norway*,
Thereto prickt on by a most emulous cause, dared to
The combate, in which our valiant *Hamlet*,
For so this side of our knowne world esteemed him,
Did slay this Fortenbrasse,
Who by a seale compact well ratified, by law
And heraldrie, did forfeit with his life all those
His lands which he stoode seazed of by the conqueror,
Against the which a moity competent,
Was gaged by our King:
Now sir, yong Fortenbrasse,
Of inapproved mettle hot and full,
Hath in the skirts of *Norway* here and there,
Sharkt up a sight of lawlesse Resolutes

For food and diet to some enterprise,
That hath a stomacke in't : and this (I take it) is the
Chiefe head and ground of this our watch.

Enter the Ghost.

But loe, behold, see where it comes againe,
Ile crosse it, though it blast me : stay illusion,
If there be any good thing to be done,
That may doe ease to thee, and grace to mee,
Speake to mee.
If thou art privy to thy countries fate,
Which happly foreknowing may prevent, O speake to me,
Or if thou hast extorted in thy life,
Or hoorded treasure in the wombe of earth,
For which they say you Spirites oft walke in death, speake
to me, stay and speake, speake, stoppe it *Marcellus.*

    2. Tis heere.   *exit Ghost.*

    Hor. Tis heere.

    Marc. Tis gone, O we doe it wrong, being so majesti-
call, to offer it the shew of violence,
For it is as the ayre invelmorable,
And our vaine blowes malitious mockery.

    2. It was about to speake when the Cocke crew.

    Hor. And then it faded like a guilty thing,
Upon a fearefull summons : I have heard
The Cocke, that is the trumpet to the morning,
Doth with his earely and shrill crowing throate,
Awake the god of day, and at his sound,
Whether in earth or ayre, in sea or fire,
The stravagant and erring spirite hies
To his confines, and of the trueth heereof.
This present object made probation.

    Marc. It faded on the crowing of the Cocke,
Some say, that ever gainst that season comes,
Wherein our Saviours birth is celebrated,
The bird of dawning singeth all night long,
And then they say, no spirite dare walke abroade,

[40]

The nights are wholesome, then no planet frikes,
No Fairie takes, nor Witch hath powre to charme,
So gratious, and so hallowed is that time.
    Hor. So have I heard, and doe in parte beleeve it:
But see the Sunne in russet mantle clad,
Walkes ore the deaw of yon hie mountaine top,
Breake we our watch up, and by my advise,
Let us impart what wee have seene to night
Unto yong *Hamlet* : for upon my life
This Spirite dumbe to us will speake to him:
Do you consent, wee shall acquaint him with it,
As needefull in our love, fitting our duetie?
    Marc. Lets doo't I pray, and I this morning know,
Where we shall finde him most conveniently.

Enter King, Queene, Hamlet, Leartes, Corambis,
and the two Ambassadors, with Attendants.

    King Lordes, we here have writ to *Fortenbrasse*,
Nephew to olde *Norway*, who impudent
And bed-rid, scarcely heares of this his
Nephews purpose : and Wee heere dispatch
Yong good *Cornelia*, and you *Voltemar*
For bearers of these greetings to olde
Norway, giving to you no further personall power
To businesse with the King,
Then those related articles do shew:
Farewell, and let your haste commend your dutie.
    Gent. In this and all things will wee shew our dutie.
    King. Wee doubt nothing, hartily farewel:
And now *Leartes*; what's the news with you?
You said you had a sute what i'st *Leartes*?
    Lea. My gratious Lord, your favorable licence,
Now that the funerall rites are all performed,
I may have leave to go againe to *France*,
For though the favour of your grace might stay mee,
Yet something is there whispers in my hart,

[41]

Which makes my minde and spirits bend all for *France*.

   King Have you your fathers leave, *Leartes*?

   Cor. He hath, my lord, wrung from me a forced graunt,
And I beseech you grant your Highnesse leave.

   King With all our heart, *Leartes* fare thee well.

   Lear. I in all love and dutie take my leave.

   King. And now princely Sonne *Hamlet*,   *Exit.*
What meanes these sad and melancholy moodes?
For your intent going to *Wittenberg*,
Wee hold it most unmeet and unconvenient,
Being the Joy and halfe heart of your mother.
Therefore let mee intreat you stay in Court,
All *Denmarkes* hope our coosin and dearest Sonne.

   Ham. My lord, ti's not the sable sute I weare:
No nor the teares that still stand in my eyes,
Nor the distracted haviour in the visage,
Nor all together mixt with outward semblance,
Is equall to the sorrow of my heart,
Him have I lost I must of force forgoe,
These but the ornaments and sutes of woe.

   King This shewes a loving care in you, Sonne *Hamlet*,
But you must thinke your father lost a father,
That father dead, lost his, and so shalbe untill the
Generall ending. Therefore cease laments,
It is a fault gainst heaven, fault gainst the dead,
A fault gainst nature, and in reasons
Common course most certaine,
None lives on earth, but hee is borne to die.

   Que. Let not thy mother loose her praiers *Hamlet*,
Stay here with us, go not to *Wittenberg*.

   Ham. I shall in all my best obay you madam.

   King Spoke like a kinde and a most loving Sonne,
And there's no health the King shall drinke to day,
But the great Canon to the clowdes shall tell
The rowse the King shall drinke unto Prince *Hamlet*.

          Exeunt all but Hamlet

Prince of Denmarke

Ham. O that this too much griev'd and sallied flesh
Would melt to nothing, or at the universall
Globe of heaven would turne al to a Chaos!
O God, within two months; no not two : married,
Mine uncle : O let me not thinke of it,
My fathers brother : but no more like
My father, then I to *Hercules*.
Within two months, ere yet the salt of most
Unrighteous teares had left their flushing
In her galled eyes : she married, O God, a beast
Devoyd of reason would not have made
Such speede: Frailtie, thy name is Woman,
Why she would hang on him, as if increase
Of appetite had growne by what it looked on.
O wicked wicked speede, to make such
Dexteritie to incestuous sheetes,
Ere yet the shooes were olde,
The which she followed my dead fathers corse
Like *Nyobe*, all teares : married, well it is not,
Nor it cannot come to good:
But breake my heart, for I must holde my tongue.

Enter Horatio *and* Marcellus.

Hor. Health to your Lordship.
Ham. I am very glad to see you, (Horatio) or I much
forget my selfe.
Hor. The same my Lord, and your poore servant ever.
Ham. O my good friend, I change that name with you:
but what make you from *Wittenberg Horatio?*
Marcellus.
Marc. My good Lord.
Ham. I am very glad to see you, good even sirs:
But what is your affaire in *Elsenoure?*
Weele teach you to drinke deepe ere you depart.
Hor. A trowant disposition, my good Lord.
Ham. Nor shall you make mee truster
Of your owne report against your selfe:

[43]

Sir, I know you are no trowant:
But what is your affaire in *Elsenoure?*
   Hor. My good Lord, I came to see your fathers funerall.
   Ham. O I pre thee do not mocke mee fellow studient,
I thinke it was to see my mothers wedding.
   Hor. Indeede my Lord, it followed hard upon.
   Ham. Thrift, thrift, *Horatio*, the funerall bak't meates
Did coldly furnish forth the marriage tables,
Would I had met my deerest foe in heaven
Ere ever I had seene that day *Horatio*;
O my father, my father, me thinks I see my father.
   Hor. Where my Lord?
   Ham. Why, in my mindes eye *Horatio.*
   Hor. I saw him once, he was a gallant King.
   Ham. He was a man, take him for all in all,
I shall not looke upon his like againe.
   Hor. My Lord, I thinke I saw him yesternight,
   Ham. Saw, who?
   Hor. My Lord, the King your father.
   Ham. Ha, ha, the King my father ke you.
   Hor. Ceasen your admiration for a while
With an attentive eare, till I may deliver,
Upon the witnesse of these Gentlemen
This wonder to you.
   Ham. For Gods love let me heare it.
   Hor. Two nights together had these Gentlemen,
Marcellus and *Bernardo*, on their watch,
In the dead vast and middle of the night.
Beene thus incountered by a figure like your father,
Armed to poynt, exactly *Capapea*
Appeeres before them thrise, he walkes
Before their weake and feare oppressed eies
Within his tronchions length,
While they distilled almost to gelly.
With the act of feare stands dumbe,
And speake not to him: this to mee
In dreadfull secresie impart they did.

And I with them the third night kept the watch,
Where as they had delivered forme of the thing.
Each part made true and good,
The Apparition comes : I knew your father,
These handes are not more like.

   Ham. Tis very strange.

   Hor. As I do live, my honord lord, tis true,
And wee did thinke it right done,
In our dutie to let you know it.

   Ham. Where was this?

   Mar. My Lord, upon the platforme where we watched.

   Ham. Did you not speake to it?

   Hor. My Lord we did, but answere made it none,
Yet once me thought it was about to speake,
And lifted up his head to motion,
Like as he would speake, but even then
The morning cocke crew lowd, and in all haste,
It shruncke in haste away, and vanished
Our sight.

   Ham. Indeed, indeed sirs but this troubles me:
Hold you the watch to night?

   All We do my Lord.

   Ham. Armed say ye?

   All Armed my good Lord.

   Ham. From top to toe?

   All. My good Lord, from head to foote.

   Ham. Why then saw you not his face?

   Hor. O yes my Lord, he wore his bever up.

   Ham. How look't he, frowningly?

   Hor. A countenance more in sorrow than in anger.

   Ham. Pale, or red?

   Hor. Nay, verie pal

   Ham. And fixt his eies upon you.

   Hor. Most constantly.

   Ham. I would I had beene there.

   Hor. It would a much amazed you.

   Ham. Yea very like, very like, staid it long?

Hor. While one with moderate pace
Might tell a hundred.
  Mar. O longer, longer.
  Ham. His beard was grisleld, no.
  Hor. It was as I have seene it in his life,
A sable silver.
  Ham. I wil watch to night, perchance t'wil walke againe.
  Hor. I warrant it will.
  Ham. If it assume my noble fathers person,
Ile speake to it, if hell it selfe should gape,
And bid me hold my peace, Gentlemen,
If you have hither consealed this sight,
Let it be tenible in your silence still,
And whatsoever else shall chance to night,
Give it an understanding, but no tongue,
I will requit your loves, so fare you well,
Upon the platforme, twixt eleven and twelve,
Ile visit you.
  All. Our duties to your honor.   *exeunt.*
  Ham. O your loves, your loves, as mine to you,
Farewell, my fathers spirit in Armes,
Well, all's not well. I doubt some foule play,
Would the night were come,
Till then, sit still my soule, foule deeds will rise
Though all the world orewhelme them to mens eies.   *Exit*

Enter *Leartes* and *Ofelia*.

Leart. My necessaries are inbarkt, I must aboord,
But ere I part, marke what I say to thee:
I see Prince *Hamlet* makes a shew of love
Beware *Ofelia*, do not trust his vowes,
Perhaps he loves you now, and now his tongue,
Speakes from his heart, but yet take heed my sister,
The Chariest maide is prodigall enough,
If she unmaske hir beautie to the Moone.
Vertue it selfe scapes not calumnious thoughts,

Believ't *Ofelia*, therefore keepe a loofe
Lest that he trip thy honor and thy fame.

   Ofel. Brother, to this I have lent attentive eare,
And doubt not but to keepe my honour firme,
But my deere brother, do not you
Like to a cunning Sophister,
Teach me the path and ready way to heaven,
While you forgetting what is said to me,
Your selfe, like to a carelesse libertine
Doth give his heart, his appetite at ful,
And little recks how that his honour dies.

   Lear. No, feare it not my deere *Ofelia*,
Here comes my father, occasion smiles upon a second leave.

Enter Corambis.

   Cor. Yet here *Leartes?* aboord, aboord, for shame,
The winde sits in the shoulder of your saile,
And you are staid for, there my blessing with thee
And these few precepts in thy memory.
"Be thou familiar, but by no means vulgare;
"Those friends thou hast, and their adoptions tried,
"Graple them to thee with a hoope of steele,
"But do not dull the palme with entertaine,
"Of every new unfleg'd courage,
"Beware of entrance into a quarrell; but being in,
"Beare it that the opposed may beware of thee,
"Costly thy apparrell, as thy purse can buy.
"But not exprest in fashion,
"For the apparell oft proclaimes the man.
And they of *France* of the chiefe rancke and station
Are of a most select and generall chiefe in that:
"This above all, to thy owne selfe be true,
And it must follow as the night the day,
Thou canst not then be false to any one,
Farewel, my blessing with thee.

   Lear. I humbly take my leave, farewell *Ofelia*,

[47]

And remember well what I have said to you.   *exit.*

    Ofel. It is already lock't within my hart,
And you your selfe shall keepe the key of it.

    Cor. What i'st *Ofelia* he hath saide to you?

    Ofel. Somthing touching the prince *Hamlet.*

    Cor. Mary wel thought on, t'is given me to understand,
That you have bin too prodigall of your maiden presence
Unto Prince Hamlet, if it be so,
As so tis given to mee, and that in waie of caution
I must tell you; you do not understand your selfe
So well as befits my honor, and your credite.

    Ofel. My lord, he hath made many tenders of his love
to me.

    Cor. Tenders, I, I, tenders you may call them.

    Ofel. And withall, such earnest vowes.

    Cor. Springes to catch woodcocks,
What, do not I know when the blood doth burne,
How prodigall the tongue lends the heart vowes,
In briefe, be more scanter of your maiden presence,
Or tendring thus you'l tender mee a foole.

    Ofel. I shall obay my lord in all I may.

    Cor. *Ofelia*, receive none of his letters,
"For lovers lines are snares to intrap the heart;
"Refuse his tokens, both of them are keyes
To unlocke Chastitie unto Desire;
Come in *Ofelia*, such men often prove,
"Great in their wordes, but little in their love.

    Ofel. I will my lord.   *exeunt.*

        Enter Hamlet, Horatio *and* Marcellus.

    Ham. The ayre bites shrewd; it is an eager and
An nipping winde, what houre i'st?

    Hor. I think it lacks of twelve,   *Sound Trumpets.*

    Mar. No, t'is strucke.

    Hor. Indeed I heard it not, what doth this mean my lord?

    Ham. O the king doth wake to night, & takes his rowse,
Keepe wassel, and the swaggering up–spring reeles,

And as he dreames, his draughts of renish downe,
The kettle, drumme, and trumpet, thus bray out,
The triumphes of his pledge.

    Hor. Is it a custome here?

    Ham. I mary i'st and though I am
Native here, and to the maner borne,
It is a custome, more honourd in the breach,
Then in the observance.

Enter the Ghost.

    Hor. Looke my Lord, it comes.

    Ham. Angels and Ministers of grace defend us,
Be thou a spirite of health, or goblin damn'd,
Bring with thee ayres from heanen, or blasts from hell:
Be thy intents wicked or charitable,
Thou commest in such questionable shape,
That I will speake to thee,
Ile call thee *Hamlet*, King, Father, Royall Dane,
O answere mee, let mee not burst in ignorance,
But say why thy canonizd bones hearsed in death
Have burst their ceremonies : why thy Sepulcher,
In which wee saw thee quietly interr'd,
Hath burst his ponderous and marble Jawes,
To cast thee up againe: what may this meane,
That thou, dead corse, againe in compleate steele,
Revissets thus the glimses of the Moone,
Making night hideous, and we fooles of nature,
So horridely to shake our disposition,
With thoughts beyond the reaches of our soules?
Say, speake, wherefore, what may this meane?

    Hor. It beckons you, as though it had something
To impart to you alone.

    Mar. Looke with what courteous action
It waves you to a more removed ground,
But do not go with it.

    Hor. No, by no meanes my Lord.

    Ham. It will not speake, then will I follow it.

[49]

Hor. What if it tempt you toward the flood my Lord.
That beckles ore his bace, into the sea,
And there assume some other horrible shape,
Which might deprive your soveraigntie of reason,
And drive you into madnesse : thinke of it.
    Ham. Still am I called, go on, ile follow thee.
    Hor. My Lord, you shall not go.
    Ham. Why what should be the feare?
I do not set my life at a pinnes fee,
And for my soule, what can it do to that?
Being a thing immortall, like it selfe,
Go on, ile follow thee.
    Mar. My Lord be rulde, you shall not goe.
    Ham. My fate cries out, and makes each pety Artive
As hardy as the Nemeon Lyons nerve,
Still am I cald, unhand me gentlemen;
By heaven ile make a ghost of him that lets me,
Away I say, go on, ile follow thee.
    Hor. He waxeth desperate with imagination.
    Mar. Something is rotten in the state of *Denmarke.*
    Hor. Have after; to what issue will this sort?
    Mar. Let's follow, tis not fit thus to obey him.   *exit.*

Enter Ghost and Hamlet.

    Ham. Ile go no farther, whither wilt thou leade me?
    Ghost Marke me.
    Ham. I will.
    Ghost I am thy fathers spirit, doomd for a time
To walke the night, and all the day
Confinde in flaming fire,
Till the foule crimes done in my dayes of Nature
Arepurged and burnt away.
    Ham. Alas poore Ghost.
    Ghost Nay pitty me not, but to my unfolding
Lend thy listning eare, but that I am forbid
To tell the secrets of my prison house

[50]

Prince of Denmarke

I would a tale unfold, whose lightest word
Would harrow up thy soule, freeze thy yong blood,
Make thy two eyes like stars start from their spheres,
Thy knotted and combined locks to part,
And each particular haire to stand on end
Like quils upon the fretfull Porpentine,
But this same blazon must not be, to eares of flesh and blood
Hamlet, if ever thou didst thy deere father love.
    Ham. O God.
    Ghost Revenge his foule, and most unnaturall murder:
    Ham. Murder.
    Ghost Yea, murder in the highest degree,
As in the least tis bad,
But mine most foule, beastly, and unnaturall.
    Ham. Haste me to knowe it, that with wings as swift as
meditation, or the thought of it, may sweepe to my revenge.
    Gho. O I finde thee apt, and duller shouldst thou be
Then the fat weede which rootes it selfe in ease
On *Lethe* wharffe : briefe let me be.
Tis given out, that sleeping in my orchard,
A Serpent stung me; so the whole eare of *Denmarke*
Is with a forged Prosses of my death rankely abusde:
But know thou noble Youth : he that did sting
Thy fathers heart, now weares his Crowne.
    Ham. O my prophetike soule, my uncle! my uncle!
    Ghost Yea he, that incestuous wretch, wonne to his will
    with gifts,
O wicked will, and gifts! that have the power
So to seduce my most seeming vertuous Queene,
But vertne, as it never will be moved,
Though Lewdnesse court it in a shape of heaven,
So Lust, though to a radiant angle linckt,
Would sate it selfe from a celestiall bedde,
And prey on garbage : but soft, me thinkes
I sent the mornings ayre, briefe let me be,
Sleeping within my Orchard, my custome alwayes
In the after noone, upon my secure houre

Thy uncle came, with juyce of Hebona
In a viall, and through the porches of my eares
Did powre the leaprous distilment, whose effect
Hold such an enmitie with blood of man,
That swift as quickesilner, it posteth through
The naturall gates and allies of the body,
And turnes the thinne and wholesome blood
Like eager dropings into milke.
And all my smoothe body, barked, and tetterd over.
Thus was I sleeping by a brothers hand
Of Crowne, of Queene, of life, of dignitie
At once deprived, no reckoning made of,
But sent unto my grave,
With all my accompts and sinnes upon my head,
O horrible, most horrible!
   Ham. O God!
   ghost If thou hast nature in thee, beare it not,
But howsoever, let not thy heart
Conspire against thy mother aught,
Leave her to heaven,
And to the burthen that her conscience beares.
I must be gone, the Glo-worme shewes the Martin
To be neere, and gin's to pale his uneffectuall fire:
Hamlet adue, adue, adue : remember me.   *Exit*
   Ham. O all you hoste of heaven! O earth, what else?
And shall I couple hell; remember thee?
Yes thou poore Ghost; from the tables
Of my memorie, ile wipe away all sawes of Bookes,
All triviall fond conceites
That ever youth, or else observance noted,
And thy remembrance, all alone shall sit.
Yes, yes, by heaven, a damnd pernitious villaine,
Murderons, bawdy, smiling damned villaine,
(My tables) meet it is I set it downe;
That one may smile, and smile, and be a villayne;
At least I am sure, it may be so in *Denmarke*.
So uncle, there you are, there you are.

Now to the words; it is adue adue : remember me,
Soe t'is enough I have sworne.

  Hor. My lord, my lord.   *Enter. Horatio,*
  Mar. Lord Hamlet.   *and Marcellus.*
  Hor. Ill, lo; lo, ho, ho.
  Mar. Ill, lo, lo, so, ho, so, come boy, come.
  Hor. Heavens secure him.
  Mar. How i'st my noble lord?
  Hor. What news my lord?
  Ham. O wonderfull, wonderful.
  Hor. Good my lord tel it.
  Ham. No not I, you'l reveale it.
  Hor. Not I my Lord by heaven.
  Mar. Nor I my Lord.
  Ham. How say you then? would hart of man
Once thinke it? but you'l be secret.
  Both. I by heaven, my lord.
  Ham. There's never a villaine dwelling in all *Denmarke*,
But hee's an arrant knave.
  Hor. There need no Ghost come from the grave to tell
you this.
  Ham. Right, you are in the right, and therefore
I holde it meet without more circumstance at all,
Wee shake hands and part; you as your busines
And desiers shall leade you : for looke you,
Every man hath busines, and desires, such
As it is, and for my owne poore parte, ile go pray.
  Hor. These are but wild and wherling words, my Lord.
  Ham. I am sory they offend you; hartely, yes faith hartily.
  Hor. Ther's no offence my Lord.
  Ham. Yes, by Saint *Patrike* but there is *Horatio*,
And much offence too, touching this vision,
It is an honest ghost, that let mee tell you,
For your desires to know what is betweene us,
Or'emaister it as you may:
And now kind frends, as yon are frends,
Schollers and gentlmen,

[53]

Grant mee one poore request.
   Both. What i'st my Lord?
   Ham. Never make known what you have seene to night
   Both. My lord, we will not.
   Ham. Nay but sweare.
   Hor. In faith my Lord not I.
   Mar. Nor I my Lord in faith.
   Ham. Nay upon my sword, indeed upon my sword.
   Gho. Sweare.

The Gost under the stage.

   Ham Ha, ha, come you here, this fellow in the sellerige,
Here consent to sweare.
   Hor. Propose the oth my Lord.
   Ham. Never to speake what you have seene to night,
Sweare by my sword.
   Gost. Sweare.
   Ham. Hic & ubique; nay then weele shift our ground:
Come hither Gentlemen, and lay your handes
Againe upon this sword, never to speake
Of that which you have seene, sweare by my sword.
   Ghost Sweare.
   Ham. Well said old Mole, can'st worke in the earth?
so fast, a worthy Pioner, once more remove.
   Hor. Day and night, but this is wondrous strange.
   Ham. And therefore as a stranger give it welcome,
There are more things in heaven and earth *Horatio*,
Then are Dream't of, in your philosophie,
But come here, as before you never shall
How strange or odde soere I beare my selfe,
As I perchance hereafter shall thinke meet,
To put an Anticke disposition on,
That you at such times seeing me, never shall
With Armes, incombred thus, or this head shake,
Or by pronouncing some undoubtfull phrase,
As well well, wee know, or wee could and if we would,
Or there be, and if they might, or such ambiguous:

Giving out to note, that you know aught of mee,
This not to doe, so grace, and mercie
At your most need helpe you, sweare
    Ghost. Sweare.
    Ham. Rest, rest, perturbed spirit: so gentleman,
In all my love I do commend mee to you,
And what so poore a man as *Hamlet* may,
To pleasure you, God willing shall not want,
Nay come lett's go together,
But stil your fingers on your lippes I pray,
The time is out of joynt, O cursed spite,
That ever I was borne to set it right,
Nay come lett's go together.   *Exeunt.*

        Enter Corambis, and Montano.

    Cor. Montano, here, these letter to my sonne,
And this same mony with my blessing to him,
And bid him ply his learning good *Montano.*
    Mon. I will my lord.
    Cor. You shall do very well *Montano,* to say thus,
I knew the gentleman, or know his father,
To inquire the manner of his life,
As thus; being amongst his acquaintance,
You may say, you saw him at such a time, marke you mee,
At game, or drincking, swearing, or drabbing,
You may go so farre.
    Mon. My Lord, that will impeach his reputation.
    Cor. I faith not a whit, no not a whit,
Now happely hee closeth with you in the consequence,
As you may bridle it not disparage him a jote.
What was I about to say,
    Mon. He closeth with him in the consequence.
    Cor. I, you say right, he closeth with him thus,
This will hee say, let mee see what hee will say,
Mary this, I saw him yesterday, or tother day,
Or then, or at such a time, a dicing,

Or at Tennis, I or drincking drunke, or entring
Of a howse of lightnes viz. brothell,
Thus sir do wee that know the world, being men of reach,
By indirections, finde directions forth,
And so shall you my sonne; you ha me, ha you not?
    Mon. I have my lord.
    Cor. Wel, fare you well, commend mee to him.
    Mon. I will my lord.
    Cor. And bid him ply his musicke
    Mon. My lord I wil.   *exit.*

Enter, Ofelia.

    Cor. Farewel, how now *Ofelia*, what's the news with you?
    Ofe. O my deare father, such a change in nature,
So great an alteration in a Prince,
So pitifull to him, fearefull to mee,
A maidens eye ne're looked on.
    Cor. Why what's the matter my *Ofelia*?
    Of. O yong Prince *Hamlet*, the only floure of *Denmark*,
Hee is bereft of all the wealth he had,
The Jewell that ador'nd his feature most
Is filcht and stolne away, his wit's bereft him,
Hee found mee walking in the gallery all alone,
There comes hee to mee, with a distracted looke,
His garters lagging downe, his shooes untide,
And fixt his eyes so stedfast on my face,
As if they had vow'd, this is their latest object.
Small while he stoode, but gripes me by the wrist,
And there he holdes my pulse till with a sigh
He doth unclaspe his holde, and parts away
Silent, as is the mid time of the night:
And as he went, his eie was still on mee,
For thus his head over his shoulder looked,
He seemed to finde the way without his eies:
For out of doores he went without their helpe,
And so did leave me.
    Cor. Madde for thy love,

[56]

What have you given him any crosse wordes of late?
   Ofelia I did repell his letters, deny his gifts,
As you did charge me.
   Cor. Why that hath made him madde:
By heav'n t'is as proper for our age to cast
Beyond our selves, as t'is for the yonger sort
To leave their wantonnesse. Well, I am sory
That I was so rash : but what remedy?
Lets to the King, this madnesse may proove,
Though wilde a while, yet more true to thy love.   *exeunt.*

   Enter King and Queene, Rossencraft, and Gilderstone.

   King Right noble friends, that our deere cosin Hamlet
Hath lost the very heart of all his sence,
It is most right, and we most sory for him:
Therefore we doe desire, even as you tender
Our care to him, and our great love to you,
That you will labour but to wring from him
The cause and ground of his distemperancie.
Doe this, the king of *Denmarke* shal be thankefull.
   Ros. My Lord, whatsoever lies within our power
Your majestie may more commaund in wordes
Then use perswasions to your liege men, bound
By love, by duetie, and obedience.
   Guil. What we may doe for both your Majesties
To know the griefe troubles the Prince your sonne,
We will indevour all the best we may,
So in all duetie doe we take our leave.
   King Thankes Guilderstone, and gentle Rossencraft.
   Que. Thankes Rossencraft, and gentle Gilderstone.

   Enter Corambis and Ofelia.

   Cor. My Lord, the Ambassadors are joyfully
Return'd from *Norway*.
   King Thou still hast beene the father of good news.
   Cor. Have I my Lord? I assure your grace,

The Tragedie of Hamlet

I holde my duetie as I holde my life,
Both to my God, and to my soveraigne King:
And I beleeve, or else this braine of mine
Hunts not the traine of policie so well
As it had wont to doe, but I have found
The very depth of Hamlets lunacie.
    Queene God graunt he hath.

Enter the Ambassadors.

    King Now *Voltemar*, what from our brother *Norway?*
    Volt. Most faire returnes of greetings and desires,
Upon our first he sent forth to suppresse
His nephews levies, which to him appear'd
To be a preparation gainst the Polacke:
But better look't into, he truely found
It was against your Highnesse, whereat grieved,
That so his sickenesse, age, and impotence,
Was falsely borne in hand, sends out arrests
On *Fortenbrasse*, which he in briefe obays,
Receives rebuke from *Norway* : and in fine,
Makes vow before his uncle, never more
To give the assay of Armes against your Majestie,
Whereon olde *Norway* overcome with joy,
Gives him three thousand crownes in annuall fee,
And his Commission to employ those souldiers,
So levied as before, against the Polacke,
With an intreaty heerein further shewne,
That it would please you to give quiet passe
Through your dominions, for that enterprise
On such regardes of safety and allowances
As therein are set downe.
    King It likes us well, and at fit time and leasure
Weele reade and answere these his Articles,
Meane time we thanke you for your well
Tooke labour : go to your rest, at night weele feast togither:
Right welcome home.   *exeunt Ambassadors.*
    Cor. This busines is very well dispatched.

Now my Lord, touching the yong Prince Hamlet,
Certaine it is that hee is madde: mad let us grant him then:
Now to know the cause of this effect,
Or else to say the cause of this defect,
For this effect defective comes by cause.
    Queene Good my Lord be briefe.
    Cor. Madam I will: my Lord, I have a daughter,
Have while shee's mine : for that we thinke
Is surest, we often loose : now to the Prince.
My Lord, but note this letter,
The which my daughter in obedience
Deliver'd to my handes.
    King Reade it my Lord.
    Cor. Marke my Lord.
Doubt that in earth is fire,
Doubt that the starres doe move,
Doubt trueth to be a liar,
But doe not doubt I love.
To the beautifull *Ofelia*:
Thine ever the most unhappy Prince *Hamlet*.
My Lord, what doe you thinke of me?
I, or what might you thinke when I sawe this?
    King As of a true friend and a most loving subject.
    Cor. I would be glad to proove so.
Now when I saw this letter, thus I bespake my maiden:
Lord *Hamlet* is a Prince out of your starre,
And one that is unequall for your love:
Therefore I did commaund her refuse his letters,
Deny his tokens, and to absent her selfe.
Shee as my childe obediently obey'd me.
Now since which time, seeing his love thus cross'd,
Which I tooke to be idle, and but sport,
He straitway grew into a melancholy,
From that unto a fast, then unto distraction,
Then into a sadnesse, from that unto a madnesse,
And so by continuance, and weakenesse of the braine
Into this frensie, which now possesseth him:

[59]

And if this be not true, take this from this.

   King Thinke you t'is so?

   Cor. How? so my lord, I would very faine know
That thing that I have saide t'is so, positively,
And it hath fallen out otherwise.
Nay, if circumstances leade me on,
Ile finde it out, if it were hid
As deepe as the centre of the earth.

   King. how should wee trie this same?

   Cor. Mary my good lord thus,
The Princes walke is here in the galery,
There let *Ofelia*, walke untill hee comes:
Your selfe and I will stand close in the study,
There shall you heare the effect of all his hart,
And if it prove any otherwise then love,
Then let my censure faile an other time.

   King. see where hee comes poring uppon a booke.

Enter Hamlet.

   Cor. Madame, will it please your grace
To leave us here?

   Que. With all my hart.   *exit.*

   Cor. And here *Ofelia*, reade you on this booke,
And walke aloofe, the King shal be unseene.

   Ham. To be, or not to be, I there's the point,
To Die, to sleep, is that all? I all:
No, to sleepe, to dreame, I mary there it goes,
For in that dreame of death, when wee awake,
And borne before an everlasting Judge,
From whence no passenger ever retur'nd,
The undiscovered country, at whose sight
The happy smile, and the accursed damn'd.
But for this, the joyfull hope of this,
Whol'd beare the scornes and flattery of the world,
Scorned by the right rich, the rich curssed of the poore?
The widow being oppressed, the orphan wrong'd,
The taste of hunger, or a tirants raigne,

And thousand more calamities besides,
To grunt and sweate under this weary life,
When that he may his full *Quietus* make,
With a bare bodkin, who would this indure,
But for a hope of something after death?
Which pusles the braine, and doth confound the sence,
Which makes us rather beare those evilles we have,
Than flie to others that we know not of.
I that, O this conscience makes cowardes of us all,
Lady in thy orizons, be all my sinnes remembred.

 Ofel. My Lord, I have sought opportunitie, which now
I have, to redeliver to your worthy handes, a small remembrance, such tokens which I have received of you.

 Ham. Are you faire?

 Ofel. My Lord.

 Ham. Are you honest?

 Ofel. What meanes my Lord?

 Ham. That if you be faire and honest,
Your beauty should admit no discourse to your honesty.

 Ofel. My Lord, can beauty have better priviledge than
with honesty?

 Ham. Yea mary may it; for Beauty may transforme
Honesty, from what she was into a bawd:
Then Honesty can transforme Beauty:
This was sometimes a Paradox,
But now the time gives it scope.
I never gave you nothing.

 Ofel. My Lord, you know right well you did,
And with them such earnest vowes of love,
As would have moov'd the stoniest breast alive,
But now too true I finde,
Rich giftes waxe poore, when givers grow unkinde.

 Ham. I never loved you.

 Ofel. You made me beleeve you did.

 Ham. O thou shouldst not a beleeved me!
Go to a Nunnery goe, why shouldst thou
Be a breeder of sinners? I am my selfe indifferent honest,

[61]

But I could accuse my selfe of such crimes
It had beene better my mother had ne're borne me,
O I am very prowde, ambitious, disdainefull,
With more sinnes at my becke, then I have thoughts
To put them in, what should such fellowes as I
Do, crawling between heaven and earth?
To a Nunnery goe, we are arrant knaves all,
Beleeve none of us, to a Nunnery goe.

    Ofel. O heavens secure him!

    Ham. Wher's thy father?

    Ofel. At home my lord.

    Ham. For Gods sake let the doores be shut on him,
He may play the foole no where but in his
Owne house : to a Nunnery goe.

    Ofel. Help him good God.

    Ham. If thou dost marry, Ile give thee
This plague to thy dowry:
Be thou as chaste as yce, as pure as snowe,
Thou shalt not scape calumny, to a Nunnery goe.

    Ofel. Alas, what change is this?

    Ham. But if thou wilt needes marry, marry a foole,
For wisemen know well enough,
What monsters you make of them, to a Nunnery goe.

    Ofel. Pray God restore him.

    Ham. Nay, I have heard of your paintings too,
God hath given you one face,
And you make your selves another,
You fig, and you amble, and you nickname Gods creatures,
Making your wantonnesse, your ignorance,
A Pox, t'is scurvy, Ile no more of it,
It hath made me madde : Ile no more marriages,
All that are married but one, shall live,
The rest shall keepe as they are, to a Nunnery goe,
To a Nunnery goe.   *exit.*

    Ofe. Great God of heaven, what a quicke change is this?
The Courtier, Scholler, Souldier, all in him,
All dasht and splinterd thence, O woe is me,

[62]

To a seene what I have seene, see what I see.   *exit.*

King Love? No, no, that's not the cause,   *Enter King and*
Some deeper thing it is that troubles him.   *Corambis.*

    Cor. Wel, something it is : my Lord, content you a while,
I will my selfe goe feele him : let me worke,
Ile try him every way : see where he comes,
Send you those Gentlemen, let me alone
To finde the depth of this, away, be gone.   *exit King.*
Now my good Lord, do you know me?   *Enter Hamlet.*

    Ham. Yea very well, y'are a fishmonger.

    Cor. Not I my Lord.

    Ham. Then sir, I would you were so honest a man,
For to be honest, as this age goes,
Is one man to be pickt out of tenne thousand.

    Cor. What doe you reade my Lord?

    Ham. Wordes, wordes.

    Cor. What's the matter my Lord?

    Ham. Betweene who?

    Cor. I meane the matter you reade my Lord.

    Ham. Mary most vile heresie:
For here the Satyricall Satyre writes,
That olde men have hollow eyes, weake backes,
Grey beardes, pitifull weake hammes, gowty legges,
All which sir, I most potently beleeve not:
For sir, your selfe shalbe olde as I am,
If like a Crabbe, you could goe backeward.

    Cor. How pregnant his replies are, and full of wit:
Yet at first he tooke me for a fishmonger:
All this comes by love, the vemencie of love,
And when I was yong, I was very idle,
And suffered much extasie in love, very neere this:
Will you walke out of the aire my Lord?

    Ham. Into my grave.

    Cor. By the masse that's out of the aire indeed,
Very shrewd answers,
My Lord I will take my leave of you.

[63]

The Tragedy of Hamlet

Enter Gilderstone, and Rossencraft.

Ham. You can take nothing from me sir,
I will more willingly part with all,
Olde doating foole.

   Cor. You seeke Prince Hamlet, see, there he is.   *exit.*

   Gil. Health to your Lordship.

   Ham. What, Gilderstone, and Rossencraft,
Welcome kinde schoole-fellowes to *Elsanoure.*

   Gil. We thanke your Grace, and would be very glad
You were as when we were at *Wittenberg.*

   Ham. I thanke you, but is this visitation free of
Your selves, or were you not sent for?
Tell me true, come, I know the good King and Queene
Sent for you, there is a kinde of confession in your eye:
Come, I know you were sent for.

   Gil. What say you?

   Ham. Nay then I see how the winde sits.
Come, you were sent for.

   Ross. My lord, we were and willingly if we might,
Know the cause and ground of your discontent.

   Ham. Why I want preferment,

   Ross. I thinke not so my lord.

   Ham. Yes faith, this great world you see contents me not,
No nor the spangled heavens, nor earth, nor sea,
No nor Man that is so glorious a creature,
Contents not me, no nor woman too, though you laugh.

   Gil. My lord, we laugh not at that.

   Ham. Why did you laugh then,
When I said, Man did not content mee?

   Gil. My Lord, we laughed, when you said, Man did not
content you.
What entertainement the Players shall have,
We boorded them a the way : they are comming to you.

   Ham. Players, what Players be they?

   Ross. My Lord, the Tragedians of the Citty,
Those that you tooke delight to see so often.

Ham. How comes it that they travell? Do they grow restie?

Gil. No my Lord, their reputation holds as it was wont.

Ham. How then?

Gil. Yfaith my Lord, noveltie carries it away,
For the principall publike audience that
Came to them, are turned to private playes,
And to the humour of children.

Ham. I doe not greatly wonder of it,
For those that would make mops and moes
At my uncle, when my father lived,
Now give a hundred, two hundred pounds
For his picture : but they shall be welcome,
He that playes the King shall have tribute of me,
The ventrous Knight shall use his foyle and target,
The lover shall sigh gratis,
The clowne shall make them laugh
That are tickled in the lungs, or the blanke verse shall halt for't,
And the Lady shall have leave to speake her minde freely.

The Trumpets sound,   *Enter Corambis.*

Do you see yonder great baby?
He is not yet out of his swadling clowts.

Gil. That may be, for they say an olde man
Is twice a childe.

Ham. Ile prophecie to you, hee comes to tell mee a the
Players,
You say true, a monday last, t'was so indeede.

Cor. My lord, I have news to tell you.

Ham. My Lord, I have newes to tell you:
When *Rossios* was an Actor in *Rome.*

Cor. The Actors are come hither, my lord.

Ham. Buz, buz.

Cor. The best Actors in Christendome,
Either for Comedy, Tragedy, Historie, Pastorall,
Pastorall, Historicall, Historicall, Comicall,
Comicall historicall, Pastorall, Tragedy historicall:
Seneca cannot be too heavy, nor *Plato* too light:

[65]

For the law hath writ those are the onely men.

   Ham. O Jepha Judge of *Israel!* what a treasure hadst thou?

   Cor. Why what a treasure had he my lord?

   Ham. Why one faire daughter, and no more,

The which he loved passing well.

   Cor. A, still harping a my daughter! well my Lord,

If you call me *Jepha*, I hane a daughter that

I love passing well.

   Ham. Nay that followes not.

   Cor. What followes then my Lord?

   Ham. Why by lot, or God wot, or as it came to passe,

And so it was, the first verse of the godly Ballet

Wil tel you all : for look you where my abridgement comes:

Welcome maisters, welcome all,   *Enter players.*

What my olde friend, thy face is vallanced

Since I saw thee last, com'st thou to beard me in *Denmarke?*

My yong lady and mistris, burlady but your

Ladiship is growne by the altitude of a chopine higher than you

   were:

Pray God sir your voyce, like a peece of uncurrant

Golde, be not crack't in the ring : come on maisters,

Weele even too't, like French Falconers,

Flie at any thing we see, come, a taste of your

Quallitie, a speech, a passionate speech.

   Players What speech my good lord?

   Ham. I heard thee speake a speech once,

But it was never acted : or if it were,

Never above twice, for as I remember,

It pleased not the vulgar, it was caviary

To the million : but to me

And others, that received it in the like kinde,

Cried in the toppe of their judgements, an excellent play,

Set downe with as great modestie as cunning:

One said there was no sallets in the lines to make the savory,

But called it an honest methode, as wholesome as sweete.

Come, a speech in it I chiefly remember

Was *Æneas* tale to *Dido,*

And then especially where he talkes of Princes slaughter,
If it live in thy memory beginne at this line,
Let me see.
The rugged *Pyrrus*, like th'arganian beast:
No t'is not so, it begins with *Pirrus*:
O I have it.
The rugged *Pirrus*, he whose sable armes,
Blacke as his purpose did the night resemble,
When he lay couched in the ominous horse,
Hath now his blacke and grimme complexion smeered
With Heraldry more dismall, head to foote,
Now is he totall guise, horridely tricked
With blood of fathers, mothers, daughters, sonnes,
Back't and imparched in calagulate gore,
Rifted in earth and fire, olde grandsire *Pryam* seekes:
So goe on.
   Cor. Afore God, my Lord, well spoke, and with good
accent.
   Play. Anone he finds him striking too short at Greeks,
His antike sword rebellious to his Arme,
Lies where it falles, unable to resist.
Pyrrus at *Pryam* drives, but all in rage,
Strikes wide, but with the whiffe and winde
Of his fell sword, th'unnerved father falles.
   Cor. Enough my friend, t'is too long.
   Ham. It shall to the Barbers with your beard:
A pox, hee's for a Jigge, or a tale of bawdry,
Or else he sleepes, come on to *Hecuba*, come.
   Play. But who, O who had seene the mobled Queene?
   Cor. Mobled Queene is good, faith very good.
   Play. All in the alarum and feare of death rose up,
And o're her weake and all ore-teeming loynes, a blancket
And a kercher on that head, where late the diademe stoode,
Who this had seene with tongue invenom'd speech,
Would treason have pronounced,
For if the gods themselves had seene her then,
When she saw *Pirrus* with malitious strokes,

[67]

Mincing her husbandes limbs,
It would have made milch the burning eyes of heaven,
And passion in the gods.

   Cor. Looke my lord if he hath not changde his colour,
And hath teares in his eyes : no more good heart, no more.

   Ham. T'is well, t'is very well, I pray my lord,
Will you see the Players well bestowed,
I tell you they are the Chronicles
And briefe abstracts of the time,
After your death I can tell you,
You were better have a bad Epiteeth,
Then their ill report while you live.

   Cor. My lord, I will use them according to their deserts.

   Ham. O farre better man, use every man after his deserts,
Then who should scape whipping?
Use them after your owne honor and dignitie,
The lesse they deserve, the greater credit's yours.

   Cor. Welcome my good fellowes.   *exit.*

   Ham. Come hither maisters, can you not play the murder of *Gonsago*?

   players Yes my Lord.

   Ham. And could'st not thou for a neede study me
Some dozen or sixteene lines,
Which I would set downe and insert?

   players Yes very easily my good Lord.

   Ham. T'is well, I thanke you : follow that lord:
And doe you heare sirs? take heede you mocke him not.
Gentlemen, for your kindnes I thanke you,
And for a time I would desire you leave me.

   Gil. Our love and duetie is at your commaund.

Exeunt all but Hamlet.

   Ham. Why what a dunghill idiote slave am I?
Why these Playeres here draw water from eyes:
For Hecuba, why what is Hecuba to him, or he to Hecuba?
What would he do and if he had my losse?
His father murdred, and a Crowne bereft him,

[68]

He would turne all his teares to droppes of blood,
Amaze the standers by with his laments,
Strike more then wonder in the judiciall eares,
Confound the ignorant, and make mute the wise,
Indeede his passion would be generall.
Yet I like to an asse and John a Dreames,
Having my father murdred by a villaine,
Stand still, and let it passe, why sure I am a coward:
Who pluckes me by the beard, or twites my nose,
Give's me the lie i'th throate downe to the lungs,
Sure I should take it, or else I have no gall,
Or by this I should a fatted all the region kites
With this slaves offell, this damned villaine,
Treacherous, bawdy, murderous villaine:
Why this is brave, that I the sonne of my deare father,
Should like a scalion, like a very drabbe
Thus raile in wordes. About my braine,
I have heard that guilty creatures sitting at a play,
Hath, by the very cunning of the scene, confest a murder
Committed long before.
This spirit that I have seene may be the Divell,
And out of my weakenesse and my melancholy,
As he is very potent with such men,
Doth seeke to damne me, I will have sounder proofes,
The play's the thing,
Wherein I'le catch the conscience of the King.   *exit.*

Enter the King, Queene, and Lordes.

King Lordes, can you by no meanes finde
The cause of our sonne Hamlets lunacie?
You being so neere in love, even from his youth,
Me thinkes should gaine more than a stranger should.

    Gil. My lord, we have done all the best we could,
To wring from him the cause of all his griefe,
But still he puts us off, and by no meanes
Would make an answere to that we exposde.

[69]

Ross. Yet was he something more inclin'd to mirth
Before we left him, and I take it,
He hath given order for a play to night,
At which he craves your highnesse company.

King With all our heart, it likes us very well:
Gentlemen, seeke still to increase his mirth,
Spare for no cost, our coffers shall be open,
And we unto your selves will still be thankefull.

Both In all wee can, be sure you shall commaund.

Queene Thankes gentlemen, and what the Queene of
Denmarke
May pleasure you, be sure you shall not want.

Gil. Weele once againe unto the noble Prince.

King Thanks to you both : Gertred you'l see this play.

Queene My lord I will, and it joyes me at the soule
He is inclin'd to any kinde of mirth.

Cor. Madame, I pray be ruled be me:
And my good Soveraigne, give me leave to speake,
We cannot yet finde out the very ground
Of his distemperance, therefore
I holde it meete, if so it please you,
Else they shall not meete, and thus it is.

King What i'st *Corambis*?

Cor. Mary my good lord this, soone when the sports are
done,
Madam, send you in haste to speake with him,
And I my selfe will stand behind the Arras,
There question you the cause of all his griefe,
And then in love and nature unto you, hee'le tell you all:
My Lord, how thinke you on't?

King It likes us well, Gerterd, what say you?

Queene With all my heart, soone will I send for him.

Cor. My selfe will be that happy messenger,
Who hopes his griefe will be reveal'd to her.   *exeunt omnes*

Enter Hamlet and the Players.

Ham. Pronounce me this speech trippingly a the tongue
as I taught thee,
Mary and you mouth it, as a many of your players do
I'de rather heare a towne bull bellow,
Then such a fellow speake my lines.
Nor do not saw the aire thus with your hands,
But give every thing his action with temperance.
O it offends mee to the soule, to heare a rebustious periwig
    fellow,
To teare a passion in totters, into very ragges,
To split the eares of the ignoraut, who for the
Most parte are capable of nothing but dumbe shewes and
    noises,
I would have such a fellow whipt, for o're doing, tarmagant
It out, Herodes Herod.
    players My Lorde, wee have indifferently reformed that
among us.
    Ham. The better, the better, mend it all together:
There be fellowes that I have seene play,
And heard others commend them, and that highly too,
That having neither the gate of Christian, Pagan,
Nor Turke, have so strutted and bellowed,
That you would a thought, some of Natures journeymen
Had made men, and not made them well,
They imitated humanitie, so abhominable:
Take heede, avoyde it.
    players I warrant you my Lord.
    Ham. And doe you heare? let not your Clowne speake
More then is set downe, there be of them I can tell you
That will laugh themselves, to set on some
Quantitie of barren spectators to laugh with them,
Albeit there is some necessary point in the Play
Then to be observed: O t'is vile, and shewes
A pittifull ambition in the foole that useth it.
And then you have some agen, that keepes one sute
Of jeasts, as a man is knowne by one sute of
Apparell, and Gentlemen quotes his jeasts downe

In their tables, before they come to the play, as thus:
Cannot you stay till I eate my porrige? and, you owe me
A quarters wages : and, my coate wants a cullison:
And, your beere is sowre : and, blabbering with his lips,
And thus keeping in his cinkapase of jeasts,
When, God knows, the warme Clowne cannot make a jest
Unlesse by chance, as the blinde man catcheth a hare:
Maisters tell him of it.

   players We will my Lord.
   Ham. Well, goe make you ready.   *exeunt players.*
   Horatio. Heere my Lord.
   Ham. Horatio, thou art even as just a man,
As e're my conversation cop'd withall.
   Hor. O my lord!
   Ham. Nay why should I flatter thee?
Why should the poore be flattered?
What gaine should I receive by flattering thee,
That nothing hath but thy good minde?
Let flattery sit on those time-pleasing tongs,
To glose with them that loves to heare their praise,
And not with such as thou *Horatio*.
There is a play to night, wherein one Sceane they have
Comes very neere the murder of my father,
When thou shalt see that Act afoote,
Marke thou the King, doe but observe his lookes,
For I mine eies will rivet to his face:
And if he doe not bleach, and change at that,
It is a damned ghost that we have seene.
Horatio, have a care, observe him well.
   Hor. My lord, mine eies shall still be on his face,
And not the smallest alteration
That shall appeare in him, but I shall note it.
   Ham. Harke, they come,

     Enter King, Queene, Corambis, and other Lords.

King How now son *Hamlet*, how fare you, shall we have
a play?

Ham. Yfaith the Camelions dish, not capon cramm'd, feede
feede a the ayre.
I father : My lord, you playd in the Universitie.
    Cor. That I did my L: and I was counted a good actor.
    Ham. What did you enact there?
    Cor. My lord, I did act *Julius Caesar*, I was killed
in the Capitoll, *Brutus* killed me.
    Ham. It was a brute parte of him,
To kill so capitall a calfe.
Come, be these Players ready?
    Queene Hamlet come sit downe by me.
    Ham. No by my faith mother, heere's a mettle more
attractive:
Lady will you give me leave, and so forth:
To lay my head in your lappe?
    Ofel. No my Lord.
    Ham. Upon your lap, what do you thinke I meant contrary
matters?

    Enter in a Dumbe Shew, the King and the Queene, he sits
      downe in an Arbor, she leaves him : Then enters Luci-
    anus with poyson in a Viall, and powres it in his eares, and
        goes away : Then the Queene commeth and findes
          him dead : and goes away with the other.

    Ofel. What meanes this my Lord?   *Enter the Prologue.*
    Ham. This is myching Mallico, that meanes my chiefe.
    Ofel. What doth this meane my lord?
    Ham. you shall heare anone, this fellow will tell you all.
    Ofel. Will he tell us what this shew meanes?
    Ham. I, or any shew you'le shew him,
Be not afeard to shew, hee'le not be afeard to tell:
O these Players cannot keepe counsell, thei'le tell all.
    Prol. For us, and for our Tragedie,
Heere stowpiug to your clemencie,
We begge your hearing patiently.
    Ham. I'st a prologue, or a poesie for a ring?

[73]

Ofel. T'is short my Lord.
Ham. As womens love.

Enter the Duke and Dutchesse.

Duke Full fortie yeares are past, their date is gone,
Since happy time joyn'd both our hearts as one:
And now the blood that fill'd my youthfull veines,
Runnes weakely in their pipes, and all the straines
Of musicke, which whilome pleasde mine eare,
Is now a burthen that Age cannot beare:
And therefore sweete Nature must pay his due,
To heaven must I, and leave the earth with you.
Dutchesse O say not so, lest that you kill my heart,
When death takes you, let life from me depart.
Duke Content thy selfe, when ended is my date,
Thon maist (perchance) have a more noble mate,
More wise, more youthfull, and one.
Dutchesse O speake no more, for then I am accurst,
None weds the second, but she kils the first:
A second time I kill my Lord that's dead,
When second husband kisses me in bed.
Ham. O wormewood, wormewood!
Duke I doe beleeve you sweete, what now you speake,
But what we doe determine oft we breake,
For our demises stil are overthrowne,
Our thoughts are ours, their end's none of our owne:
So thinke you will no second husband wed,
But die thy thoughts, when thy first Lord is dead.
Dutchesse Both here and there pursue me lasting strife,
If once a widdow, ever I be wife.
Ham. If she should breake now.
Duke T'is deepely sworne, sweete leave me here a while,
My spirites growe dull, and faine I would beguile the tedi-
ous time with sleepe.
Dutchesse Sleepe rocke thy braine,
And never come mischance betweene us twaine.   *exit Lady*

[74]

Ham. Madam, how do you like this play?

Queene The Lady protests too much.

Ham. O but shee'le keepe her word.

King Have you heard the argument, is there no offence
in it?

Ham. No offence in the world, poyson in jest, poison in jest.

King What do you call the name of the play?

Ham. Mouse-trap: mary how trapically : this play is
The image of a murder done in *guyana, Albertus*
Was the Dukes name, his wife *Baptista,*
Father, it is a knavish peece a worke : but what
A that, it toucheth not us, you and I have free
Soules, let the galld jade wince, this is one
Lucianus nephew to the King.

Ofel. Ya're as good as a *Chorus* my lord.

Ham. I could interpret the love you beare, if I sawe the
poopies dallying.

Ofel. Y'are very pleasant my lord.

Ham. Who I, your onlie jig-maker, why what shoulde
a man do but be merry? for looke how cheerefully my mother lookes, my father died within these two houres.

Ofel. Nay, t'is twice two months, my Lord.

Ham. Two months, nay then let the divell weare blacke,
For i'le have a sute of Sables : Jesus, two months dead,
And not forgotten yet? nay then there's some
Likelyhood, a gentlemans death may outlive memorie,
But by my faith hee must build churches then,
Or els hee must follow the olde Epitithe,
With hoh, with ho, the hobi-horse is forgot.

Ofel. Your jests are keene my Lord.

Ham. It would cost you a groning to take them off.

Ofel. Still better and worse.

Ham. So you must take your husband, begin. Murdred
Begin, a poxe, leave thy damnable faces and begin,
Come, the croking raven doth bellow for revenge.

Murd. Thoughts blacke, hands apt, drugs fit, and time
agreeing.

Confederate season, else no creature seeing:
Thou mixture rancke, of midnight weedes collected,
With *Hecates* bane thrise blasted, thrise infected,
Thy naturall magicke, and dire propertie,
One wholesome life usurps immediately.   *exit.*
   Ham. He poysons him for his estate.
   King Lights, I will to bed.
   Cor. The king rises, lights hoe.

Exeunt King and Lordes.

   Ham. What, frighted with false fires?
Then let the stricken deere goe weepe,
The Hart ungalled play,
For some must laugh, while some must weepe,
Thus runnes the world away.
   Hor. The king is mooved my lord.
   Hor. I *Horatio*, i'le take the Ghosts word
For more then all the coyne in *Denmarke*.

Enter Rossencraft and Gilderstone.

   Ross. Now my lord, how is't with you?
   Ham. And if the king like not the tragedy,
Why then belike he likes it not perdy.
   Ross. We are very glad to see your grace so pleasant,
My good lord, let us againe intreate
To know of you the ground and cause of your distemperature
   Gil. My lord, your mother craves to speake with you.
   Ham. We shall obey, were she ten times our mother.
   Ross. But my good Lord, shall I intreate thus much?
   Ham. I pray will you play upon this pipe?
   Ross. Alas my lord I cannot.
   Ham. Pray will you.
   Gil. I have no skill my Lord.
   Ham. why looke, it is a thing of nothing,
T'is but stopping of these holes,
And with a little breath from your lips,

It will give most delicate musick.

   Gil. But this cannot wee do my Lord.

   Ham. Pray now, pray hartily, I beseech you.

   Ros. My lord wee cannot.

   Ham. Why how unworthy a thing would you make of me?
You would seeme to know my stops, you would play upon
   mee,
You would search the very inward part of my hart,
And dive into the secreet of my soule.
Zownds do you thinke I am easier to be pla'yd
On, then a pipe? call mee what Instrument
You will, though you can frett mee, yet you can not
Play upon mee, besides, to be demanded by a spunge.

   Ros. How a spunge my Lord?

   Ham. I sir, a spunge, that sokes up the kings
Countenance, favours, and rewardes, that makes
His liberalitie your store house : but such as you,
Do the king, in the end, best servise;
For he doth keep you as an Ape doth nuttes,
In the corner of his Jaw, first mouthes you,
Then swallowes you : so when hee hath need
Of you, t'is but squeesing of you,
And spunge, you shall be dry againe, you shall.

   Ros. Wel my Lord wee'le take our leave.

   Ham Farewell, farewell, God blesse you.

        Exit Rossencraft and Gilderstone.

           Enter Corambis

   Cor. My lord, the Queene would speake with you.

   Ham. Do you see yonder clowd in the shape of a camell?

   Cor. T'is like a camell in deed.

   Ham. Now me thinkes it's like a weasel.

   Cor. T'is back't like a weasell.

   Ham. Or like a whale.

   Cor. Very like a whale.   *exit Coram.*

[77]

The Tragedie of Hamlet

Ham. Why then tell my mother i'le come by and by.
Good night Horatio.

   Hor. Good night unto your Lordship.   *exit Horatio.*

   Ham. My mother she hath sent to speake with me:
O God, let ne're the heart of *Nero* enter
This soft bosome.
Let me be cruell, not unnaturall.
I will speake daggers, those sharpe wordes being spent,
To doe her wrong my souls shall ne're consent.   *exit.*

Enter the King.

   Kin O that this wet that falles upon my face
Would wash the crime cleere from my conscience!
When I looke up to heaven, I see my trespasse,
The earth doth still crie out upon my fact,
Pay me the murder of a brother and a king,
And the adulterous fault I have committed:
O these are sinnes that are unpardonable:
Why say thy sinnes were blacker then is jeat,
Yet may contrition make them as white as snowe:
I but still to persever in a sinne,
It is an act gainst the universall power,
Most wretched wan, stoope, bend thee to thy prayer,
Aske grace of heaven to keepe thee from despaire.

hee kneeles.   enters Hamlet

   Ham. I so, come forth and worke thy last,
And thus hee dies : and so am I revenged:
No, not so : he tooke my father sleeping, his sins brim full,
And how his soule stoode to the state of heaven
Who knowes, save the immortall powres,
And shall I kill him now,
When he is purging of his soule?
Making his way for heaven, this is a benefit,
And not revenge : no, get thee up agen,

[78]

When hee's at game swaring, taking his carowse, drinking
 drunke,
Or in the incestuous pleasure of his bed,
Or at some act that hath no relish
Of salvation in't, then trip him
That his heeles may kicke at heaven,
And fall as lowe as hel : my mother stayes,
This phisicke but prolongs thy weary dayes.   *exit Ham.*
  King My wordes fly up, my sinnes remaine below.
No King on earth is safe, if Gods his foe.   *exit King.*

Enter Queene and Corambis.

  Cor. Madame, I heare yong Hamlet comming,
I'le shrowde my selfe behinde the Arras.   *exit Cor.*
  Queene Do so my Lord.
  Ham. Mother, mother, O are you here?
How is't with you mother?
  Queene How is't with you?
  Ham. I'le tell you, but first weele make all safe.
  Queene Hamlet, thou hast thy father much offended.
  Ham. Mother, you have my father much offended.
  Queene How now boy?
  Ham. How now mother! come here, sit downe, for you
shall heare me speake.
  Queene What wilt thou doe? thou wilt not murder me:
Helpe hoe.
  Cor. Helpe for the Queene.
  Ham. I a Rat, dead for a Duckat.
Rash intruding foole, farewell,
I tooke thee for thy better.
  Queene Hamlet, what hast thou done?
  Ham. Not so much harme, good mother,
As to kill a king, and marry with his brother.
  Queene How! kill a king!
  Ham. I a King : nay sit you downe, and ere you part,
If you be made of penitrable stuffe,
I'le make your eyes looke downe into your heart,

And see how horride there and blacke it shews.

    Queene Hamlet, what mean'st thou by these killing words?

    Ham. Why this I meane, see here, behold this picture,
It is the portraiture, of your deceased husband,
See here a face, to outface *Mars* himselfe,
An eye, at which foes did tremble at,
A front wherin all vertues are set downe
For to adorne a king, and guild his crowne,
Whose heart went hand in hand even with that vow,
He made to you in marriage, and he is dead.
Murdred, damnably murdred, this was your husband,
Looke you now, here is your husband,
With a face like *Vulcan*.
A looke fit for a murder and a rape,
A dull dead hanging looke, and a hell-bred eie,
To affright children and amaze the world:
And this same have you left to change with this.
What Divell thus hath cosoned you at hob-man blinde?
A! have you eyes and can you looke on him
That slew my father, and your deere husband,
To live in the incestuous pleasure of his bed?

    Queene O Hamlet, speake no more.

    Ham. To leave him that bare a Monarkes minde,
For a king of clowts, of very shreads.

    Queene Sweete Hamlet cease.

    Ham. Nay but still to persist and dwell in sinne,
To sweate under the yoke of infamie,
To make increase of shame, to seale damnation.

    Queene Hamlet, no more.

    Ham. Why appetite with you is in the waine,
Your blood runnes backeward now from whence it came,
Who'le chide hote blood within a Virgins heart,
When lust shall dwell within a matrons breast?

    Queene Hamlet, thou cleaves my heart in twaine.

    Ham. O throw away the worser part of it, and keepe the
better.

Prince of Denmarke

Enter the ghost in his night gowne.

Save me, save me, you gratious
Powers above, and hover over mee,
With your celestiall wings.
Doe you not come your tardy sonne to chide,
That I thus long have let revenge slippe by?
O do not glare with lookes so pittiful!
Lest that my heart of stone yeelde to compassion,
And euery part that should assist revenge,
Forgoe their proper powers, and fall to pitty.
     Ghost Hamlet, I once againe appeare to thee,
To put thee in remembrance of my death:
Doe not neglect, nor long time put it off.
But I perceive by thy distracted lookes,
Thy mother's fearefull, and she stands amazde:
Speake to her Hamlet, for her sex is weake,
Comfort thy mother, Hamlet, thinke on me.
     Ham. How is't with you Lady?
     Queene Nay, how is't with you
That thus you bend your eyes on vacancie,
And holde discourse with nothing but with ayre?
     Ham. Why doe you nothing heare?
     Queene Not I.
     Ham. Nor doe you nothing see?
     Queene No neither.
     Ham. No, why see the king my father, my father, in the
habite
As he lived, looke you how pale he lookes,
See how he steales away out of the Portall,
Looke, there he goes.   *exit ghost.*
     Queene Alas, it is the weakenesse of thy braine,
Which makes thy tongue to blazon thy hearts griefe:
But as I have a soule, I sweare by heaven,
I never knew of this most horride murder:
But Hamlet, this is onely fantasie,
And for my love forget these idle fits.

[81]

The Tragedie of Hamlet

Ham. Idle, no mother, my pulse doth beate like yours,
It is not madnesse that possesseth Hamlet.
O mother, if ever you did my deare father love,
Forbeare the adulterous bed to night,
And win your selfe by little as you may,
In time it may be you will lothe him quite:
And mother, but assist mee in revenge,
And in his death your infamy shall die.

Queene Hamlet, I vow by that majesty,
That knowes our thoughts, and lookes into our hearts,
I will conceale, consent, and doe my best,
What stratagem soe're thou shalt devise.

Ham. It is enough, mother good night:
Come sir, I'le provide for you a grave,
Who was in life a foolish prating knave.

Exit Hamlet with the dead body.

Enter the King and Lordes

King Now Gertred, what sayes our sonne, how doe you
finde him?

Queene Alas my lord, as raging as the sea:
Whenas he came, I first bespake him faire,
But then he throwes and tosses me about,
As one forgetting that I was his mother:
At last I call'd for help : and as I cried, *Corambis*
Call'd, which Hamlet no sooner heard, but whips me
Out his rapier, and cries, a Rat, a Rat, and in his rage
The good olde man he killes.

King Why this his madnesse will undoe our state.
Lordes goe to him, inquire the body out.

Gil. We will my Lord.   *Exeunt Lordes.*

King Gertred, your sonne shall presently to England,
His shipping is already furnished,
And we have sent by *Rossencraft* and *Gilderstone*,
Our letters to our deare brother of England,
For Hamlets welfare and his happinesse:

[82]

Happly the aire and climate of the Country
May please him better than his native home:
See where he comes.

Enter Hamlet and the Lordes.

Gil. My lord, we can by no meanes
Know of him where the body is.
 King Now sonne Hamlet, where is this dead body?
 Ham. At supper, not where he is eating, but
Where he is eaten, a certaine company of politicke wormes
 are even now at him.
Father, your fatte King, and your leane Beggar
Are but variable services, two dishes to one messe:
Looke you, a man may fish with that worme
That hath eaten of a King.
And a Beggar eate that fish,
Which that worme hath caught.
 King What of this?
 Ham. Nothing father, but to tell you, how a King
May go a progresse through the guttes of a Beggar.
 King But sonne *Hamlet*, where is this body?
 Ham. In heav'n, if you chance to miss him there,
Father, you had best looke in the other partes below
For him, and if you cannot finde him there,
You may chance to nose him as you go up the lobby.
 King Make haste and finde him out.
 Ham. Nay doe you heare? do not make too much haste,
I'le warrant you hee'le stay till you come.
 King Well sonne *Hamlet*, we in care of you: but specially
in tender preservation of your health,
The which we price even as our proper selfe,
It is our minde you forthwith goe for *England*,
The winde sits faire, you shall aboorde to night,
Lord *Rossencraft* and *Gilderstone* shall goe along with you.
 Ham. O with all my heart: farewell mother.
 King Your loving father, *Hamlet*.
 Ham. My mother I say : you married my mother,

[83]

My mother is your wife, man and wife is one flesh,
And so (my mother) farewel : for England hoe.

exeunt all but the king.

  king Gertred, leave me,
And take your leave of *Hamlet*,
To England is he gone, ne're to returne:
Our Letters are unto the King of England,
That on the sight of them, on his allegeance,
He presently without demaunding why,
That *Hamlet* loose his head, for he must die,
There's more in him than shallow eyes can see:
He once being dead, why then our state is free.   *exit.*

Enter Fortenbrasse, Drumme and Souldiers.

  Fort. Captaine, from us goe greete
The king of Denmarke:
Tell him that *Fortenbrasse* nephew to old *Norway*,
Craves a free passe and conduct over his land,
According to the Articles agreed on:
You know our Randevous, goe march away.   *exeunt all.*

enter King and Queene.

  King Hamlet is ship't for England, fare him well,
I hope to heare good newes from thence ere long,
If every thing fall out to our content,
As I doe make no doubt but so it shall.
  Queene God grant it may, heav'ns keep my *Hamlet* safe:
But this mischance of olde *Corambis* death,
Hath piersed so the yong *Ofeliaes* heart,
That she, poore maide, is quite bereft her wittes.
  King Alas deere heart! And on the other side,
We understand her brother's come from *France*,
And he hath halfe the heart of all our Land,
And hardly hee'le forget his fathers death,
Unlesse by some meanes he be pacified.

[84]

Qu. O see where the yong *Ofelia* is!

*Enter Ofelia playing on a Lute, and her haire
downe singing.*

Ofelia How should I your true love know
From another man?
By his cockle hatte, and his staffe,
And his sandall shoone.
White his shrowde as mountaine snowe,
Larded with sweete flowers,
That bewept to the grave did not goe
With true lovers showers:
He is dead and gone Lady, he is dead and gone,
At his head a grasse greene turffe,
At his heeles a stone.
   king How i'st with you sweete *Ofelia*?
   Ofelia Well God yeeld you,
It grieves me to see how they laid him in the cold ground,
I could not chuse but weepe:
And will he not come againe?
And will he not come againe?
No, no, hee's gone, and we cast away mone,
And he never will come againe.
His beard as white as snowe:
All flaxen was his pole,
He is dead, he is gone,
And we cast away moane:
God a mercy on his soule.
And of all christen soules I pray God.
God be with you Ladies, God be with you.   *exit Ofelia.*
   king A pretty wretch! this is a change indeede:
O Time, how swiftly runnes our joyes away?
Content on earth was never certaine bred,
To day we laugh and live, to morrow dead.
How now, what noyse is that?

A noyse within.   enter Leartes.

Lear. Stay there untill I come,
O thou vilde king, give me my father:
Speake, say, where's my father?
   king Dead.
   Lear. Who hath murdred him? speake, i'le not
Be juggled with, for he is murdred.
   Queene True, but not by him.
   Lear. By whome, by heav'n I'le be resolved.
   king Let him go *Gertred*, away, I feare him not,
There's such divinitie doth wall a king,
That treason dares not looke on.
Let him goe *Gertred*, that your father is murdred,
T'is true, and we most sory for it,
Being the chiefest piller of our state:
Therefore will you like a most desperate gamster,
Swoop-stake-like, draw at friend, and foe, and all?
   Lear. To his good friends thus wide I'le ope mine arms,
And locke them in my hart, but to his foes,
I will no reconcilement but by bloud.
   king Why now you speake like a most loving sonne:
And that in soule we sorrow for for his death,
Your selfe ere long shall be a witnesse,
Meane while be patient, and content your selfe.

Enter Ofelia as before.

   Lear. Who's this, *Ofelia?* O my deere sister!
I'st possible a yong maides life,
Should be as mortall as an olde mans sawe?
O heav'ns themselves! how now *Ofelia?*
   Ofel. Wel God a mercy, I a bin gathering of floures:
Here, here is rew for you,
You may call it hearb a grace a Sundayes,
Heere's some for me too: you must weare your rew
With a difference, there's a dazie.
Here Love, there's rosemary for you
For remembrance : I pray Love remember,
And there's pansey for thoughts.

[86]

Lear. A document in madnes, thoughts, remembrance:
O God, O God!

Ofelia There is fennell for you, I would a giv'n you
Some violets, but they all withered, when
My father died : alas, they say the owle was
A Bakers daughter, we see what we are,
But can not tell what we shall be.
For bonny sweete Robin is all my joy.

    Lear. Thoughts & afflictions, torments worse than hell.

    Ofel. Nay Love, I pray you make no words of this now:
I pray now, you shall sing a downe,
And you a downe a, t'is a the Kings daughter
And the false steward, and if any body
Aske you of any thing, say you this.
To morrow is saint Valentines day,
All in the morning betime,
And a maide at your window,
To be your Valentine:
The yong man rose, and dan'd his clothes,
And dupt the chamber doore,
Let in the maide, that out a maide
Never departed more.
Nay I pray marke now,
By gisse, and by saint Charitie,
Away, and fie for shame:
Yong men will doo't when they come too't
By cocke they are too blame.
Quoth she, before you tumbled me,
You promised me to wed.
So would I a done, by yonder Sunne,
If thou hadst not come to my bed.
So God be with you all, God bwy Ladies.
God bwy you Love.   *exit Ofelia.*

    Lear. Griefe upon griefe, my father murdered,
My sister thus distracted:
Cursed be his soule that wrought this wicked act.

    king Content you good Leartes for a time,
Although I know your griefe is as a floud,

Brimme full of sorrow, but forbeare a while,
And thinke already the revenge is done
On him that makes you such a haplesse sonne.
   Lear. You have prevail'd my Lord, a while I'le strive,
To bury griefe within a tombe of wrath,
Which once unhearsed, then the world shall heare
Leartes had a father he held deere.
   king No more of that, ere many dayes be done,
You shall heare that you do not dream upon.   *exeunt om.*

Enter Horatio and the Queene.

   Hor. Madame, your sonne is safe arriv'de in *Denmarke*,
This letter I even now receiv'd of him,
Whereas he writes how he escap't the danger,
And subtle treason that the king had plotted,
Being crossed by the contention of the windes,
He found the Packet sent to the king of *England*,
Wherein he saw himselfe betray'd to death,
As at his next conversion with your grace,
He will relate the circumstance at full.
   Queene Then I perceive there's treason in his lookes
That seem'd to sugar o're his villanie:
But I will soothe and please him for a time,
For murderous mindes are alwayes jealous,
But know not you *Horatio* where he is?
   Hor. Yes Madame, and he hath appoynted me
To meete him on the east side of the Cittie
To morrow morning.
   Queene O faile not, good *Horatio*, and withall, commend me
A mothers care to him, bid him a while
Be wary of his presence, lest that he
Faile in that he goes about.
   Hor. Madam, never make doubt of that:
I thinke by this the news be come to court:
He is arriv'de, observe the king, and you shall
Quickely finde, *Hamlet* being here,
Things fell not to his minde.
   Queene But what became of *Gilderstone* and *Rossencraft*?

[88]

Hor. He being set ashore, they went for *England,*
And in the Packet there writ down that doome
To be perform'd on them poynted for him:
And by great chance he had his fathers Seale,
So all was done without discoverie.

    Queene Thankes be to heaven for blessing of the prince,
Horatio once againe I take my leave,
With thowsand mothers blessings to my sonne.

    Horat. Madam adue.

Enter King and Leartes.

    King. Hamlet from *England!* is it possible?
What chance is this? they are gone, and he come home.

    Lear. O he is welcome, by my soule he is:
At it my jocund heart doth leape for joy,
That I shall live to tell him, thus he dies.

    king Leartes, content your selfe, be rulde by me,
And you shall have no let for your revenge.

    Lear. My will, not all the world.

    King Nay but Leartes, marke the plot I have layde,
I have heard him often with a greedy wish,
Upon some praise that he hath heard of you
Touching your weapon, which with all his heart,
He might be once tasked for to try your cunning.

    Lea. And how for this?

    King Mary Leartes thus : I'le lay a wager,
Shalbe on *Hamlets* side, and you shall give the oddes,
The which will draw him with a more desire,
To try the maistry, that in twelve venies
You gaine not three of him : now this being granted,
When you are hot in midst of all your play,
Among the foyles shall a keene rapier lie,
Steeped in a mixture of deadly poyson,
That if it drawes but the least dramme of blood,
In any part of him, he cannot live:
This being done will free you from suspition,
And not the deerest friend that *Hamlet* lov'de
Will ever have Leartes in suspect.

Lear. My lord, I like it well:
But say lord *Hamlet* should refuse this match.
    King I'le warrant you, wee'le put on you
Such a report of singularitie,
Will bring him on, although against his will.
And lest that all should misse,
I'le have a potion that shall ready stand,
In all his heate when that he calles for drinke,
Shall be his period and our happinesse.
    Lear. T'is excellent, O would the time were come!
Here comes the Queene.   *enter the Queene.*
    king How now Gertred, why looke you heavily?
    Queene O my Lord, the yong *Ofelia*
Having made a garland of sundry sortes of floures,
Sitting upon a willow by a brooke,
The envious sprig broke, into the brooke she fell,
And for a while her clothes spread wide abroade,
Bore the yong Lady up : and there she sate smiling,
Even Mermaide-like, twixt heaven and earth,
Chaunting olde sundry tunes uncapable
As it were of her distresse, but long it could not be,
Till that her clothes, being heavy with their drinke,
Dragg'd the sweete wretch to death.
    Lear. So, she is drownde:
Too much of water hast thou Ofelia,
Therefore I will not drowne thee in my teares,
Revenge it is must yeeld this heart releefe,
For woe begets woe, and griefe hangs on griefe.   *exeunt.*

enter Clowne and an other.

    Clowne I say no, she ought not to be buried
In christian buriall.
    2. Why sir?
    Clowne Mary because shee's drownd.
    2. But she did not drowne her selfe.
    Clowne No. that's certaine, the water drown'd her.
    2. Yea but it was against her will.
    Clowne No, I deny that, for looke you sir, I stand here

If the water come to me, I drowne not my selfe:
But if I goe to the water, and am there drown'd,
Ergo I am guiltie of my owne death:
Y'are gone, goe y'are gone sir.

2. I but see, she hath christian buriall,
Because she is a great woman.

Clowne Mary more's the pitty, that great folke
Should have more authoritie to hang or drowne
Themselves, more than other people:
Goe fetch me a stope of drinke, but before thou
Goest, tell me one thing, who buildes strongest,
Of a Mason, a Shipwright, or a Carpenter?

2. Why a Mason, for he buildes all of stone,
And will indure long.

Clowne That's pretty, too't agen, too't agen.

2. Why then a Carpenter, for he buildes the gallowes,
And that brings many a one to his long home.

Clowne Pretty agen, the gallowes doth well, mary howe
dooes it well? the gallowes dooes well to them that doe ill,
goe get thee gone:
And if any one aske thee hereafter, say,
A Grave-maker, for the houses he buildes
Last till Doomes-day. Fetch me a stope of beere, goe.

Enter Hamlet and Horatio

Clowne A picke-axe and a spade,
A spade for and a winding sheete,
Most fit it is, for t'will be made,   *he throwes up a shovel.*
For such a ghest most meete.

Ham. Hath this fellow any feeling of himselfe,
That is thus merry in making of a grave?
See how the slave joles their heads against the earth.

Hor. My Lord, Custome hath made it in him seeme nothing.

Clowne A pick-axe and a spade, a spade,
For and a winding sheete,
Most fit it is for to be made,
For such a ghest most meet.

[91]

Ham. Looke you, there's another *Horatio*.
Why mai't not be the soull of some Lawyer?
Me thinkes he should indite that fellow
Of an action of Batterie, for knocking
Him about the pate with's shovel : now where is your
Quirkes and quillets now, your vouchers and
Double vouchers, your leases and free-holde,
And tenements? why that same boxe there will scarse
Holde the conveiance of his land, and must
The honor lie there? O pittifull transformance!
I prethee tell me *Horatio*,
Is parchment made of sheep-skinnes?
   Hor. I my Lorde, and of calves-skinnes too.
   Ham. Ifaith they proove themselves sheepe and calves
That deale with them, or put their trust in them.
There's another, why may not that be such a ones
Scull, that praised my Lord such a ones horse,
When he meant to beg him? *Horatio*, I prethee
Lets question yonder fellow.
Now my friend, whose grave is this?
   Clowne Mine sir.
   Ham. But who must lie in it?
   Clowne If I should say, I should, I should lie in my throat sir.
   Ham. What man must be buried here?
   Clowne No man sir.
   Ham. What woman?
   Clowne. No woman neither sir, but indeede
One that was a woman.
   Ham. An excellent fellow by the Lord *Horatio*,
This seaven yeares have I noted it : the toe of the pesant,
Comes so neere the heele of the courtier,
That he gawles his kibe, I prethee tell mee one thing,
How long will a man lie in the ground before hee rots?
   Clowne I faith sir, if hee be not rotten before
He be laide in, as we have many pocky corses,
He will last you, eight yeares, a tanner
Will last you eight yeares full out, or nine.
   Ham. And why a tanner?

Clowne Why his hide is so tanned with his trade,
That it will holde out water, that's a parlous
Devourer of your dead body, a great soaker.
Looke you, here's a scull hath been here this dozen yeare,
Let me see, I ever since our last king *Hamlet*
Slew *Fortenbrasse* in combat, yong *Hamlets* father,
Hee thats mad.

 Ham. I mary, how came he madde?
 Clowne Ifaith very strangely, by loosing of his wittes.
 Ham. Upon what ground?
 Clowne A this ground, in *Denmarke*.
 Ham. Where is he now?
 Clowne Why now they sent him to *England*.
 Ham. To *England*! wherefore?
 Clowne Why they say he shall have his wittes there,
Or if he have not, t'is no great matter there,
It will not be seene there.

 Ham. Why not there?
 Clowne Why there they say the men are as mad as he.
 Ham. Whose scull was this?
 Clowne This, a plague on him, a madde rogues it was,
He powred once a whole flagon of Rhenish of my head,
Why do not you know him? this was one *Yorickes* scull.

 Ham. Was this? I prethee let me see it, alas poore *Yoricke*
I knew him *Horatio*,
A fellow of infinite mirth, he hath caried mee twenty times
upon his back, here hung those lippes that I have Kissed a
hundred times, and to see, now they abhorre me : Wheres
your jests now *Yoricke?* your flashes of meriment : now go
to my Ladies chamber, and bid her paint her selfe an inch
thicke, to this she must come *Yoricke. Horatio,* I prethee tell
me one thing, doost thou thinke that *Alexander* looked thus?

 Hor. Even so my Lord.
 Ham. And smelt thus?
 Hor. I my lord, no otherwise.
 Ham. No, why might not imagination worke, as thus of
Alexander, Alexander died, *Alexander* was buried, *Alexander*

[93]

became earth, of earth we make clay, and *Alexander* being
but clay, why might not time bring to passe, that he might
stoppe the boung hole of a beere barrell?
Imperious *Cesar* dead and turnd to clay,
Might stoppe a hole, to keepe the winde away

Enter King and Queene, Leartes, and other lordes,
with a Priest after the coffin.

Ham. What funerall's this that all the Court laments?
It shews to be some noble parentage:
Stand by a while.
   Lear. What ceremony else? say, what ceremony else?
   Priest My Lord, we have done all that lies in us,
And more than well the church can tolerate,
She hath had a Dirge sung for her maiden soule:
And but for favour of the king, and you,
She had beene buried in the open fieldes,
Where now she is allowed christian buriall.
   Lear. So, I tell thee churlish Priest, a ministring Angell
shall my sister be, when thou liest howling.
   Ham. The faire *Ofelia* dead!
   Queene Sweetes to the sweete, farewell:
I had thought to adorne thy bridale bed, faire maide,
And not to follow thee unto thy grave.
   Lear. Forbeare the earth a while : sister farewell:

Leartes leapes into the grave.

Now powr your earth on, *Olympus* hie,
And make a hill to o're top olde *Pellon*:   *Hamlet leapes*
Whats he that conjures so?   *in after Leartes*
   Ham. Beholde tis I, *Hamlet* the Dane.
   Lear. The divell take thy soule.
   Ham. O thou praiest not well,
I prethee take thy hand from off my throate,
For there is something in me dangerous,
Which let thy wisedome feare, holde off thy hand:

[94]

Prince of Denmarke

I lov'de *Ofelia* as deere as twenty brothers could:
Shew me what thou wilt doe for her:
Wilt fight, wilt fast, wilt pray,
Wilt drinke up vessels, eate a crocadile? Ile doot:
Com'st thou here to whine?
And where thou talk'st of burying thee a live,
Here let us stand : and let them throw on us,
Whole hills of earth, till with the heighth therof,
Make Oosell as a Wart.
     King. Forbeare *Leartes*, now is hee mad, as is the sea,
Anone as milde and gentle as a Dove:
Therefore a while give his wilde humour scope.
     Ham. What is the reason sir that you wrong mee thus?
I never gave you cause : but stand away,
A Cat will meaw, a Dog will have a day.

Exit Hamlet and Horatio.

     Queene. Alas, it is his madnes makes him thus,
And not his heart, *Leartes.*
     King. My lord, t'is so : but wee'le no longer trifle,
This very day shall *Hamlet* drinke his last,
For presently we meane to send to him,
Therfore *Leartes* be in readynes.
     Lear. My lord, till then my soule will not bee quiet.
     King. Come *Gertred*, wee'l have *Leartes*, and our sonne,
Made friends and Lovers, as befittes them both,
Even as they tender us, and love their countrie.
     Queene God grant they may.   *exeunt omnes.*

Enter Hamlet and Horatio

     Ham. beleeve mee, it greeves me much *Horatio*,
That to *Leartes* I forgot my selfe:
For by my selfe me thinkes I feel his griefe,
Though there's a difference in each others wrong.

[95]

Enter a Bragart Gentleman.

Horatio, but marke yon water-flie,
The Court knowes him, but hee knowes not the Court.
  Gent. Now God save thee, sweete prince *Hamlet*.
  Ham. And you sir: foh, how the muske-cod smels!
  Gen. I come with an embassage from his majesty to you
  Ham. I shall sir give you attention:
By my troth me thinkes t'is very colde.
  Gent. It is indeede very rawish colde.
  Ham. T'is hot me thinkes.
  Gent. Very swoltery hote:
The King, sweete Prince, hath layd a wager on your side,
Six Barbary horse, against six french rapiers,
With all their acoutrements too, a the carriages:
In good faith they are very curiously wrought.
  Ham. The cariages sir, I do not know what you meane.
  Gent. The girdles, and hangers sir, and such like.
  Ham. The worde had beene more cosin german to the
phrase, if he could have carried the canon by his side,
And howe's the wager? I understand you now.
  Gent. Mary sir, that yong Leartes in twelve venies
At rapier and Dagger do not get three oddes of you,
And on your side the King hath laide,
And desires you to be in readinesse.
  Ham. Very well, if the King dare venture his wager,
I dare venture my skull : when must this be?
  Gent. My Lord, presently, the king, and her majesty,
With the rest of the best judgement in the Court,
Are comming downe into the outward pallace.
  Ham. Goe tell his majesty, I wil attend him.
  Gent. I shall deliver your most sweet answer.   *exit*.
  Ham. You may sir, none better, for y'are spiced,
Else he had a bad nose could not smell a foole.
  Hor. He will disclose himselfe without inquirie.
  Ham. Beleeve me Horatio, my hart is on the sodaine
Very sore, all here about.

Hor. My lord, forbeare the challenge then.
Ham. No *Horatio*, not I, if danger be now,
Why then it is not to come, theres a predestiuate providence
in the fall of a sparrow : heere comes the King.

Enter King, Queene, Leartes, Lordes.

King Now sonnne *Hamlet*, we hane laid upon your head,
And make no question but to have the best.
Ham. Your majestie hath laide a the weaker side.
King We doubt it not, deliver them the foiles.
Ham. First Leartes, heere's my hand and love,
Protesting that I never wrongd *Leartes*.
If *Hamlet* in his madnesse did amisse,
That was not *Hamlet*, but his madnes did it,
And all the wrong I e're did to *Leartes*,
I here proclaime was madnes, therefore lets be at peace,
And thinke I have shot mine arrow o're the house,
And hurt my brother.
Lear. Sir I am satisfied in nature,
But in termes of honor I'le stand aloofe,
And will no reconcilement,
Till by some elder maisters of our time
I may be satisfied.
King Give them the foyles.
Ham. I'le be your foyle *Leartes*, these foyles,
Have all a laught, come on sir: *a hit.*
Lear. No none.   *Heere they play:*
Ham. Judgement.
Gent. A hit, a most palpable hit.
Lear. Well, come again.   *They play againe.*
Ham. Another. Judgement.
Lear. I, I grant, a tuch, a tuch.
King Here *Hamlet*, the king dothe drinke a health to thee
Queene Here *Hamlet*, take my napkin, wipe thy face.
King. Give him the wine.
Ham. Set it by, I'le have another bowt first,

I'le drinke anone.

    Queene Here *Hamlet*, thy mother drinkes to thee.

Shee drinkes.

    King Do not drinke *Gertred* : O t'is the poysned cup!

    Ham. Leartes come, you dally with me,

I pray you passe with your most cunningst play.

    Lear. I! say you so? have at you,

Ile hit you now my Lord:

And yet it goes almost against my conscience.

    Ham. Come on sir.

    They catch one anothers Rapiers, and both are wounded,
    Leartes falles downe, the Queene falles downe and dies.

    King Looke to the Queene.

    Queene O the drinke, the drinke, *Hamlet*, the drinke.

    Ham. Treason, ho, keepe the gates.

    Lords How ist my Lord *Leartes?*

    Lear. Even as a coxcombe should,

Foolishly slaine with my owne weapon:

Hamlet, thou hast not in thee halfe an houre of life,

The fatall Instrument is in thy hand.

Unbated and invenomed: thy mother's poysned

That drinke was made for thee.

    Ham. The poysned Instrument within my hand?

Then venome to thy venome, die damn'd villaine:

Come drinke, here lies thy union here.   *The king dies.*

    Lear. O he is justly served:

Hamlet, before I die, here take my hand,

And withall, my love : I doe forgive thee.   *Leartes dies.*

    Ham. And I thee, O I am dead *Horatio*, fare thee well.

    Hor. No, I am more an antike Roman,

Then a Dane, here is some poison left.

    Ham. Upon my love I charge thee let it goe,

O fie *Horatio*, and if thou shouldst die,

What a scandale wouldst thou leave behinde?

[98]

What tongue should tell the story of our deaths,
If not from thee? O my heart sinckes *Horatio*,
Mine eyes have lost their sight, my tongue his use:
Farewel *Horatio*, heaven receive my soule.   *Ham. dies.*

> *Enter Voltemar and the Ambassadors from England.*
> *enter Fortenbrasse with his traine.*

Fort. Where is this bloudy sight?
Hor. If aught of woe or wonder you'ld behold,
Then looke upon this tragicke spectacle.
Fort. O imperious death! how many Princes
Hast thou at one draft bloudily shot to death?
Ambass. Our ambassie that we have brought from *England*,
Where be these Princes that should heare us speak?
O most most unlooked for time! unhappy country.
Hor. Content your selves, Ile show to all, the ground,
The first beginnings of this Tragedy:
Let there a scaffold be rearde up in the market place,
And let the State of the world be there:
Where you shall heare such a sad story tolde,
That never mortall man could more unfolde.
Fort. I have some rights of memory to this kingdome,
Which now to claime my leisure doth invite mee:
Let foure of our chiefest Captaines
Beare *Hamlet* like a souldier to his grave:
For he was likely, had he lived,
To a prov'd most royall.
Take up the bodie, such a fight as this
Becomes the fieldes, but here doth much amisse.

Finis

[99]

Endnotes

Page 37

two Centinels: the guards are appropriately anonymous: not characters, but voices. The use of numbers rather than names as speech headings emphasises the priority of theatrical over literary values. All proper names appearing within the dialogue in this text are italicised as if for specific emphasis by the actor.

watch: guard.

ground: place or country.

leegemen: loyal subjects.
the Dane: the King of Denmark.

give you: God give you, I wish you.

this thing: as a sceptic, Horatio refuses to accept the reality of the ghost. The absence of any question mark at the end of his line could suggest a cynical rather than an interrogative delivery.

fantasie: imagination.

Touching: concerning.

along: to come along.

Page 38

approove: confirm.

Tut: i.e. Nonsense!

Assaile your eares: strenuously attempt to persuade you.

fortified: continuing the imagery of military assault from the previous line.

Endnotes

What: i.e. with what.

Last night of al: only last night.

his: its.

to Illumine: to light up.
The full stop between 'Illumine that part of heaven' and 'Where now it burns' is grammatically incorrect. The consequent punctuational space seems, however, to act both as a 'caesura', denoting an emphatic pause, and as an 'indexical sign', stressing a physically directed attention and preparing for the apparition of the ghost.

towling: tolling.

see where it comes: the complete absence of visual 'special effects' on the bare platform of the Jacobean public stage gives particular point to the announced entry and signalled exit of a silent character: cf. 'See, it stalkes away'.

same: i.e. the same as on the previous night.

figure: physical appearance.

horrors mee: fills me with horror.

It would be spoke to: It wants to be spoken to.

usurps the state: unlawfully assumes control of both the appearance of the dead king, and his kingdom. The allegation also alludes to the actual usurpation of the state by the dead King's brother.

Majestie of buried Denmarke: the dead King.

sometimes: formerly.

offended: perhaps, given the circumstances of old Hamlet's death, by Horatio's accusation of usurpation. The original text prints the stage direction *exit Ghost* on the same line as Marcellus' observation, indicating perhaps a simultaneity of speech and gesture.

on't: of it.

Afore my God: I swear before God.
might: could.

without the sensible and true avouch: without the undeniable evidence (true avouch) of my sense of sight.

Page 39
Norway: King of Norway. We later learn that they fought in single combat.

Endnotes

angry parle: violent parley, encounter.

smot the sleaded pollax on the yce: angrily smashed his battle-axe down on the ice. 'Sleaded' is obscure, perhaps 'leaded'.

jump: exactly.

dead hower: still, ominous hour.

Marshall stalke: military stride.

In what particular to worke, I knowe not: Horatio does not understand the object of the ghost's return.

thought and scope: general drift.

eruption: upheaval.

watch: guard.

toyles the subject: puts the subjects to toil.

why: why there is.
cost: expenditure.

forraine: foreign.
marte: market, trade.

impresse: conscription.
ship-writes: ship builders.
sore taske: heavy labour.

divide: distinguish between. The shipwrights work a seven-day week.

toward: about to happen.

whisper: rumour.

even but now: only just now.

Thereto prickt on: spurred towards it.
emulous cause: envious motive.

dared to / The combate: challenged to single combat.

Hamlet: i.e. old Hamlet, the Prince's father.

this side of our knowne world: all Europe.

Fortenbrasse: old Fortinbras, father of young Fortinbras.

seale compact: an agreement ratified by the king's seal.

heraldrie: heraldic regulations governing chivalric engagements.

Endnotes

stoode seazed of: possessed personally (i.e. not the entire country but the king's personal lands).

Against the which: Matching this.

moity competent: adequate portion.

gaged: wagered.

yong Fortenbrasse: son of old Fortinbras, the dead King of Norway.

inapproved mettle: untried or reckless courage.

skirts: outlying regions.

Sharkt up a sight of lawlesse Resolutes: gathered indiscriminately together a gang of desperate criminals.

Page 40

For food and diet: prepared to serve for subsistence wages.

stomacke: danger, opportunity to display courage.

Chiefe head and ground: main source and basis.

crosse it: cross its path (and attempt to detain it).

grace to me: bring me spiritual credit.

art privy to: have private knowledge of.

happly: haply = perhaps (with the suggestion of fortunately).

hoorded treasure in the wombe of earth: buried treasure under ground.

being so majesticall: i.e. as the ghost is so majestical in appearance.

shew: appearance.

invelmorable: invulnerable.

malitious mockery: futile evidence of ill will.

trumpet: trumpeter.

lofty: high sounding.

god of day: Phoebus Apollo, the sun god of classical mythology.
his: i.e. the cock's.

stravagant: wandering.
erring: roaming.
hies: hurries.

Endnotes

confines: place of confinement.

of the truth heerof / This present object made probation: this recent sight (of the Ghost's hurried departure) proves the truth of that superstition.

ever: always.
gainst: in preparation for.
that season: i.e. Christmas.

The bird of dawning: i.e. the cock.

abroade: i.e. outside its place of confinement.

Page 41

wholesome: healthy.
strikes: exerts evil influence.

takes: bewitches.
charme: cast spells.

so gratious and so hallowed: so filled with divine grace, and so holy.

russet mantle: reddish-brown cloak.

deaw: dew.

Break we our watch up: Let us disperse our guard.

yong Hamlet: to distinguish him from his father, old Hamlet.

writ: written.

Norway: the King of Norway.

impudent: Q1's 'impudent' is generally regarded as an error for 'impotent', which appears in the Second Quarto and Folio texts. The normal sense of 'impudent' ('shameless') does not seem to apply here; but OED records a neutral use from 1619, meaning 'free from shamefastness'. Possibly 'impervious to proper moral obligation'.

For: as.

to businesse: to negotiate.

let your haste commend your dutie: demonstrate your loyalty by making all possible speed.

Wee doubt nothing: i.e. we have no doubt at all.

sute: formal request. The more familiar spelling 'Laertes' is replaced in

Endnotes

this text by 'Leartes', which produces for the modern reader a potentially confusing speech-prefix, '*Lear*'.

licence: permission.

Page 42
Sonne: i.e. stepson.

For your intent: 'as for your intention'.

halfe heart: i.e. the Queen's love for Hamlet occupies half her heart; her love for her husband the other half.

Wittenberg: Luther had founded a university in the city in 1502.

haviour in the visage: i.e. facial expressions.

These: i.e. the external appearance of his clothes and behaviour.

loose her praiers: pray in vain.

in all my best: to the best of my abilities.

But: without.
tell: proclaim.

rowse: carouse.

Page 43
sallied: sullied.

Hercules: the hero of classical mythology.

Unrighteous: insincere.
flushing: the redness caused by the salt tears.

galled: sore.

such / Dexteritie to incestuous sheets: to slip so nimbly into another's bed. Marriage to a deceased husband's brother was widely regarded as incestuous.

followed: i.e. in the funeral procession.

Nyobe: in classical mythology, Niobe's seven sons and seven daughters were slain by Apollo and Artemis and in her grief she shed so many tears that she was turned into stone.

make you from: are you doing away from.

even: evening.

Endnotes

teach you to drinke deepe: ironically referring to the drunken behaviour of the Court.

trowant disposition: desire to play truant (from his studies at Wittenberg).

Page 44

affaire: business.

pre thee: pray thee (more familiar as 'prithee').

studient: student.

hard: closely.

coldly: as cold dishes.

deerest: closest, inveterate.

Ceasen your admiration: control your astonishment.

deliver: report.

dead vast: desolate space.

to poynt: correct in every detail.
Capapea: 'cap-a-pie', from head to foot.

feare oppressed eies: their eyes heavy and troubled with fear.

tronchions: staff's.

distilled: dissolved.
gelly: jelly.

act: effect.

dreadfull secresie: awe-struck silence.

Page 45

as they had delivered forme of the thing: exactly as they had described the appearance of the thing.

Each part made true and good: every detail of their description proved exactly correct.

These handes are not more like: i.e. not more like each other than the ghost was like your father.

right done, / In our dutie: appropriate, considering our obligations.

watched: kept guard.

Endnotes

to motion, / Like as he would speak: in a gesture apparently indicating a desire to speak.

bever: visor.

pal: pale.

constantly: unflinchingly.

a much amazed: have greatly astonished, bewildered.

very like: most likely.

Page 46

tell: count.

grisleld: grey.

sable silver: black streaked with silver-grey.

warrant: guarantee.

hither: hitherto, up to now.

let it be tenible in your silence still: let it be firmly held in your confidence.

requit: pay back, reward.

doubt: suspect.

my necessaries are inbarkt: my luggage has been loaded onto the ship.

Chariest: most modest.
prodigall enough: quite sufficiently free in exposing her beauty to the Moon.

scapes: escapes.
calumnious: slanderous.

Page 47

a loofe: aloof, keep your distance.

Sophister: sophist, casuistical reasoner.

occasion smiles upon a second leave: i.e. here is a happy opportunity to say farewell for a second time.

Yet: still.

sits in the shoulder of your saile: blows in the right direction.

staid for: being waited for.

Polonius' catechism is in this text more clearly identified, by the use of quotation marks, as a series of platitudes.

familiar: friendly.
vulgare: common.

adoptions: friendship.
tried: tested.

dull the palme: tarnish your handshake.
with entertaine: by entertaining, greeting.

unfleg'd courage: immature gallant.

entrance into: beginning.

Beare it: conduct it.

the opposed: the person you're quarrelling with.

not exprest in fashion: not of an ephemeral fashion.

station: position in society.

of a most select and general chiefe: generally acknowledged elite leaders (of fashion).

that: i.e. their choice of clothes.

Page 48

Mary: a mild oath, contracted from 'By the Virgin Mary'.

prodigall: liberal.

tis given to mee: it is suggested to me.

in waie of: in the interests of.

understand your selfe: understand your proper duty.

tenders: offers. Polonius suggests that the word might better be interpreted in its other sense of 'presentation of money', cash payment.

Springes: snares.
woodcocks: a bird proverbially easy to ensnare.

the blood doth burne: sexual passions are excited.

prodigall: lavishly.

tendring thus: (under)valuing yourself in that way, you will make me seem a fool (as father of a seduced child).

[108]

be more scanter of: be more protective of.

shrewd: sharply.

eager: bitter.

lacks of twelve: is shortly before midnight.

doth wake: stays awake.

rowse: carouse.

keeps wassel: holds a drinking party.
up-spring: riotous form of dance.

Page 49

dreames: drinks himself into a dream. Q2 has 'draines his drafts', F has 'draines his draughts'.

renish: wine from the Rhineland.

triumphes of his pledge: ceremonies to accompany the king's 'pledging'.

to the maner borne: i.e. it is part of his cultural heritage.

breach: breaking.

Be thou: whether you are.
spirite of health: good spirit.
goblin damn'd: evil demon.

Bring: whether you bring.
ayres from heanen: breezes from heaven.
blasts: blighting winds.

Be thy intents: whether your intentions are.

questionable shape: in an indeterminate form, or an appearance inviting interrogation.

canonizd: consecrated, buried.
hearsed: coffined.

ceremonies: cerements, shrouds.

interr'd: entombed.

Jawes: i.e. doors.

corse: corpse.
compleate steele: full armour.

Endnotes

Revissets: revisits.

the glimses of the moon: i.e. the earth (seen by moonlight).

fooles of nature: confounded by nature.

horridely: dreadfully.
disposition: composure.

removed ground: secluded spot.

Page 50
beckles ore his bace: 'beckles' is obscure. Perhaps related to 'beck' and meaning 'bow' or 'nod' over its base.

deprive your soveraigntie of reason: take away the sovereignty of your reason.
set: value.
pinnes fee: price of a pin.

And for: and as for.

rulde: ruled.

pety Artive: minor artery.

hardy: courageous.
Nemeon Lyons: one of Hercules' twelve labours was to kill the lion of Nemea.

lets: hinders.

waxeth: grows.

Have after: pursue him.

To what issue will this sort?: what will be the outcome of all this?

thus: in such a situation.

Marke me: pay attention.

spirit: ghost.

doomd: sentenced.

Arepurged: Are purged

Page 51
Porpentine: porcupine.

Endnotes

this same blazon must not be: no human being can contemplate so graphic a description of the horrors of purgatory.

Haste me to knowe it: Tell me immediately.

apt: fitting and ready to learn.
fat weede: perhaps the opiate effects of the poppy are alluded to, but no particular plant can be identified with certainty.

Lethe wharf: the banks of Lethe. In classical mythology, Lethe was the river which dead souls had to cross before entering Hades. Drinking the river's water was held to induce oblivion.

orchard: garden.

whole eare of Denmarke: general opinion (with an ironic anticipation of the mode of his own murder).

forged Prosses: fabricated account.

rankely abusde: grossly deceived.

vertne, as it never will: i.e. just as virtue never will.

Lewdnesse: lust.
a shape of heaven: angelic form.

sate it selfe from a celestial bedde: grow satiated with a heavenly partner.

garbage: entrails.

but soft: an exclamation commanding haste or silence.

sent: scent.

secure: free from care.

Page 52

juyce of Hebona: generic term for poison.

viall: small vessel.

leaprous distilment: distillation causing effects similar to leprosy.

quickesilner: quicksilver, mercury.

gates and allies: i.e. the veins and arteries.

eager dropings: sour additions (which curdle).

barked, and tetterd over: crusted and covered with a skin eruption.

no reckoning made of: no opportunity to render an account (of my sins).

accompts: debts (i.e. sins) – continuing the commercial imagery of 'reckoning'.

nature: natural feeling.

heaven: heaven's judgement.

Martin: morning.

gin's: begins.
his: i.e. the glow-worm's.
uneffectuall: ineffectual.

hoste of heaven: angels.

couple: include.

fond: foolish.

tables: tablets (on which information could be written and erased).

Murderons: Murderous

meet it is: it is appropriate.

there you are: i.e. I have written it down.

Page 53
Illo, lo, lo, ho, ho: in this context, simply a shouted cry to hail a distant person.

Ill, lo, lo, so, ho, so, come boy, come: Hamlet interprets Marcellus' call as that of the falconer summoning his hawk to return.

secure him: keep him from harm.

Once: ever.

But hee's: i.e. that is not.

circumstance: ceremony.

point: direct.

much offence: referring to the revelations of the ghost.

For: as for.

Or'emaister it: subdue it.

yon: you.

Endnotes

In faith . . . not I: i.e. I swear not to reveal anything.

upon my sword: because its hilt formed a cross.

sellerige: cellars. In performance the actor playing the Ghost obviously remained in the hollow space beneath the stage after his exit (perhaps through a trapdoor). Hamlet's metadramatic comedy draws attention to the voice beneath the stage, and to the movements of the actor from one side to the other.

Hic & ubique: Latin: 'here and everywhere'.

Pioner: military miner.

as a stranger give it welcome: i.e. welcome it as you would an unknown guest.

Anticke disposition: fantastic manner of behaviour.

Armes, incombred: arms folded (indicating knowledge of a secret).

undoubtfull: mysterious.

such ambiguous: these and similar ambiguous expressions.

This not to doe . . .: 'as you hope for the assistance of grace and mercy when you need them most, swear not to do this'.

what so poore a man . . .: 'you shall not lack (God willing) anything poor Hamlet may be able to do to please you'.

out of joynt: dislocated.

mony: money.

ply his learning: stick to his studies.

at game: gambling.
drabbing: whoring.

hee closeth with you . . . bridle it not disparage him a jote: 'he will become friendly with you because of what you've said, and you can control the conversation so as not to slander Leartes at all'.

men of reach: men of deep insight.

indirections: devious methods.

Endnotes

directions: true information.

you ha me: you understand me.

ply: practice.

As if they had vow'd . . . : 'as if his eyes had sworn never to look at anything but her face again'.

Page 57

t'is as proper for . . .: 'it is just as appropriate for those of my generation to seek intelligence, as it would be for the young to renounce their licentiousness'.

right: true.

tender: value.

distemperancie: malady.

tale our leave: take our leave.

still: always.

Page 58

Hunts not the traine of policie: Corambis compares his pursuit of a trail of intrigue to a hunter following the track of his prey.

first: first mention of the problem.

Polacke: Poles.

impotence: infirmity.

falsely borne in hand: abused.
arrests: orders to desist from further action.

in fine: in conclusion.

give the assay of Armes: offer combat.

fee: income.

intreaty: request.

quiet passe: free passage.

regardes of safety and allowances: conditions regarding the security of the state.

likes: pleases.

well / Tooke: well undertaken.

Page 59

   defect: a mental defect.

   for this effect defective . . .: 'this consequence – Hamlet's madness – must derive from some cause'.

   while shee's mine: while she is unmarried.

   out of your starre: too far above your social status for marriage.

   unequall: socially incompatible.

Page 60

   take this from this: probably his head from his shoulders.

   trie: investigate.

   let my censure faile: ignore my judgement.

Page 61

   may his full Quietus make: end his life.

   bare bodkin: dagger/pin.

   pusles: puzzles.

   orizons: prayers.

   admit no discourse to your honesty: permit no conversation with your honesty: i.e. beauty and honesty should not mix.

Page 62

   becke: call.

   secure: protect.

   fig: presumably an obscene quibble on the vagina.

   making your wantonnesse, your ignorance: making your ignorance an excuse for affectation.

Page 63

   feele: investigate.

   fishmonger: perhaps alluding to Polonius' role as 'bawd' to Ophelia or to the smell of corruption.

   matter . . . matter: 'subject' and 'quarrell'.

   hammes: thighs.

   pregnant: ingenious.

Endnotes

vemencie: vehemency.

extasie: madness.

out of the aire: indoors.

Page 64

with all: with.

Tragedians: actors (not necessarily of tragedies).

Page 65

travell: tour.

private playes: the more fashionable and expensive indoor 'private playhouses' began to compete with the public theatres in 1599.

children: referring to the Children of the Chapel, a company of boy actors who, for a while, rivalled the popular theatres in popularity.

mops and moes: faces.

ventrous: adventurous.
foyle and target: sword and shield.

tickled in the lungs: tickled as deep as the lungs (cf. tickled to death).

swadling clowts: baby clothes.

Rossios: Roscius, a famous actor in ancient Rome.

Buz, buz: an exclamation expressing contempt for out of date information.

Comedy, Tragedy . . .: these lines are presumably satirising both Polonius' pedantry and the elaborate generic classifications of Renaissance literary theory.

Seneca: the Roman philosopher and tragic dramatist.
Plato: [Plautus?] Roman playwright held as a model for writers of comedies.

Page 66

the law hath writ: neo-classical critical theory has declared these dramatists as the only respecters of the classical 'unities'.

Jepha: in the Old Testament, Jephthah sacrificed his daughter, having previously promised that if he were successful in battle against the Ammonites, he would offer up in sacrifice the first living thing he encountered.

passing: surpassing.

Endnotes

hane: have.

followes not: i.e. does not follow logically – but Hamlet is also referring to an old ballad on the subject of Jephthah, and Polonius' line does not follow in the ballad.

lot: chance.
wot: knows.

godly Ballet: goodly ballad.

abridgement: entertainment (i.e. the players)/excuse for interrupting this conversation.

vallanced: i.e. bearded.

beard: defy.

yong lady: a boy actor.

burlady: a mild oath, 'by our lady'.

altitude: height.
chopine: artificially raised platform soles of shoes.

uncurrant / Golde: a gold coin that was no longer legal tender because it had been 'clipped' or cracked within the 'ring' which surrounded the monarch's face.

crack't: boys could not take on women's roles after their voices had broken.

even too't: i.e. get on with the business.

French Falconers: who were regarded as indiscriminating in the way that they launched their birds at the first appearance of any prey.

Quallitie: acting skills.

caviary: caviare.
the million: the masses (who had not acquired a taste for this newly introduced and expensive import).

received: acknowledged.

Cried in the toppe of their judgements: excelled.

modestie: restraint.
cunning: skill.

sallets: salads (alluding to bawdy passages).

[117]

Endnotes

make the savory: make the lines highly spiced (and therefore 'unsavoury').

Aeneas tale to Dido: Aeneas recounted the fall of Troy to Dido in Book II of Virgil's *Aeneid*.

Page 67

rugged: shaggy, ferocious.
Pyrrus: the Greek warrior who slew Priam.
th' arganian beast: the tiger. Hyrcania, a province by the Caspian sea, was famed in antiquity for its savage tigers.

sable: black.

ominous horse: the wooden horse of Troy.

complexion: appearance.

Heraldry: armorial bearings.

totall guise . . . with blood: completely dressed, horridly spotted with blood . . .

Back't and imparched in calagulate gore: baked and encrusted with clotted blood.

Rifted: broke or belched out.

Anone: in a short while.
him: i.e. Priam.

wide: i.e. wide of the target.

fell: cruel.

Jigge: a comical performance put on at the end of some plays.

Hecuba: Priam's wife.

mobled: muffled, veiled.

alarum: commotion.

all ore-teeming: i.e. worn out with child-bearing.

with tongue invenom'd speech: i.e. with bitter speech, as from a tongue dipped in poison.

Page 68

milch: milk-producing (i.e. tearful).
burning eyes of heaven: 'would have made the sun and stars weep'.

bestowed: accommodated.

Endnotes

Chronicles: histories.

abstracts: summary.

you were better: i.e. it would be preferable to,
Epiteeth: epitaph.

after: according to.

for a neede: if necessary.

Page 69

generall: universal.

Confound: dumbfound.
the ignorant: i.e. those ignorant of the crime.

Like . . . John a Dreames: presumably a proverbial day dreamer.

Give's me the lie: calls me liar.

gall: bile, i.e. bitterness of spirit.

region kites: all the kites (a scavenging bird of prey) in the region.

brave: fine.

scalion: scullion.

drabbe: prostitute.

About: i.e. begin to work.

cunning: skilful presentation.

by no meanes . . . we exposde: would give absolutely no reply to our questions.

Page 70

what the Queene . . .: 'whatever the Queene of Denmark can do to please you . . .'

distemperance: illness, mental instability.

meete: fit, proper.

nature: natural feeling.

Page 71

a the tongue: on the tongue.

Endnotes

mouth: speak loudly.

give every thing his action: use only appropriate gestures.

rebustious periwig fellow: a loud-mouthed actor in a wig.

totters: tatters.

ignoraut: ignorant.

capable of nothing but: can understand nothing except.

tarmagant / It out, Herodes Herod: 'tarmagant' was a Moslem deity who does not figure in earlier drama. Herod was a stark ranting character in Biblical drama. Both are examples of rôles encouraging actors to display extreme histrionics.

indifferently: to some extent.

gate: walk, demeanour.

journeymen: wage-labourers.

abhominable: abominable.

sute / Of Jeasts: collection of jests.

Page 72

In their tables: in their notebooks, diaries.

Cannot you stay . . .: obviously familiar catch-phrases from contemporary comedians.

cinkapase of jeasts: comic routine. 'Cinkapase' was a dance.

warme: cheeky, saucy.

cop'd withall: met with

tongs: tongues.

glose: flatter.

Act: action (of murder) and Act (unit of dramatic performance).

afoote: in process.

bleach: turn white.

Page 73

Camelions . . . capon: chameleons . . . castrated cockerels which were 'crammed' with food before being slaughtered.

Endnotes

my L.: my Lord.

brute . . . capitall a calfe: Hamlet puns on 'Brutus' and 'Capitol'. 'Calfe' means a fool.

mettle more attractive: a more magnetic type of metal/spirit (i.e. Ofelia).

do you thinke I meant contrary matters: do you think I meant the opposite of what I said (with a pun on 'cunt').

Dumbe Shew: silent performance.

powres: pours.

myching Mallico: a piece of polyglot gibberish: 'Miching Malicho' in F, 'munching Mallico' in Q2.

my chiefe: this appears as 'mischief' in the other texts. Since 'myching Mallico' is clearly nonsense, there seems no reason why the whole sentence should not be nonsense too.

shew: exhibit your body.

Be not: as long as you are not.

keepe counsell: keep a secret.

thei'le: they'll.

stowpiug: stooping (i.e. bowing).

a poesie for a ring: motto inscribed inside a ring; i.e. too perfunctory for a Prologue.

Page 74
pipes: veins.

and one. / O speake no more: although the punctuation does not indicate an interruption, such a break between speeches is obviously intended.

wormewood: a bitter tasting plant.

demises: legal term for the transference of property, etc.; here 'intentions'.

die thy thoughts: your intentions will die.

breake: i.e. break her vow.

sleepe. / Sleepe rock thy brain: although there is no indication in the punctuation, this reads as a cue for the Duke to fall asleep: 'when sleepe . . . [*falls asleep*]'. 'Sleepe rock thy braine . . .'.

[121]

Endnotes

offence: offensive material.

offence: Hamlet puns on offence = crime.

Mouse-trap: i.e. a trap set to 'catch the conscience of the King'.

trapically: i.e. the title is derived from a trope, a figure of speech, and the action takes place in a tropical location ('*guyana*'). The other texts print 'tropically'. The word also puns on 'trap'.

image: representation.

free: innocent.

galld jade: saddle-sore horse of inferior quality.
wince: kick out.

If I saw the poopies dallying: Hamlet imagines himself as a puppet master providing the voices of the 'dallying' puppets.

onlie jig-maker: the only person who's creating entertainment.

Sables: made from the fur of the sable.

the old Epitithe . . .: a common allusion to the folklore figure of the 'hobby-horse'.

keene: sharp-witted, bitter.

groning: cries of a virgin losing her maidenhead.
to take them off: to take off his keen edge, i.e. to blunt his sexual desire (misinterpreting Ophelia's 'keene').

Still better, and worse: still wittier and more obscene.

So you must take your husband: i.e. for better or worse, as in the marriage service.

a poxe: an oath: 'a pox on you'.

the croking raven doth bellow for revenge: Hamlet quotes loosely from an old play, the anonymous *True Tragedy of Richard III*.

Confederate season: i.e. opportune moment.
else no creature seeing: i.e. no one else being present to observe.

midnight: alluding to the belief that poisonous plants gathered at midnight were particularly potent.

Endnotes

Hecate's bane: Hecate's poison (Hecate was the goddess of witchcraft).

dire propertie: dreadful powers.

for: i.e. to gain.

estate: i.e. his position and possessions.

false fires: blank shot / fireworks.

stricken: wounded.

Hart ungalled: unwounded stag.

Hor: since Horatio is addressed here, the lines must be assigned to Hamlet.

perdy: by God.

distemperature: illness, anger.

Page 77

unworthy a thing: i.e. of less complexity than a pipe: 'since you cannot play that, but you think you can 'play' (manipulate) me'.

frett: irritate/finger (as on the fretboard of an instrument).

Tis back't: has a back (although a weasel's back bears no similarity to that of a camel).

Page 78

Nero: the Roman emperor famed for his cruelty who arranged for the murder of his own mother.

fact: deed.

Pay me: punishes me for.

jeat: jet.

wan: man (the 'm' is printed upside down).

game swaring: uttering oaths in the course of gambling.

Page 79

carowse: carouse.

This phisicke: i.e. Claudius' prayers (spiritual medicine which cannot cure, but has prolonged life by persuading Hamlet to delay his revenge).

dead for a Duckat: i.e. I wager a ducat he is dead.

better: social superior (i.e. the King).

penitrable: capable of being penetrated (by emotions).

Endnotes

Mars: god of war.

guild: gild.

Vulcan: Roman god, a brilliant but deformed craftsman.

murder: murderer.

rape: rapist.
What Divell thus hath cosoned you at hob-man blinde?: what devil has cheated you in a game of blind man's buff?

a king of clowts, of very shreads: a king of rags and tatters.

waine: wane.

runnes backeward: in the opposite direction (from when you were young).

Enter the ghost in his night gowne: since darkness could not be represented on the Elizabethan stage, a space of daylight performance, night was signalled conventionally by actors wearing night attire, carrying candles, appearing with disordered hair, etc. The theatrical convention explains what would otherwise seem an oddity – why would a *ghost* wear a *night gown*?

bend: direct.
vacancie: empty space.

habite: clothing.

Portall: doorway.

blazon: express.

if ever you did my deare father love: echoing the Ghost's words to Hamlet – see above, p. 51.

win your selfe by little: gradually distance yourself.

And mother, but assist mee in revenge . . .: this indication of collusion between Hamlet and Gertred appears only in this text.

politicke: political/scheming.

even now at him: i.e. are eating him even at this moment.

Endnotes

variable service: various dishes of food.

to one messe: i.e. but each is consumed by the same diners (worms).

progresse: official journey.

nose: smell.

price: prize.

Page 84

passe: passage.

Randevous: rendezvous.

piersed: pierced.

bereft her wittes: has lost her wits.

halfe the heart: half the loyalty, popular affection.

Page 85

cockle hatte, and his staffe: suggesting the dress of a pilgrim, symbol of a courtly lover.

shoone: shoes.

Larded: decorated.

God yeeld you: thank you (God yield = reward you).

mone: moan.

pole: poll (head).

never certaine bred: not born to be reliable.

Page 86

vilde: vile.

juggled with: manipulated, cheated.

such divinitie . . .: a King is protected by divine right.

piller: pillar.

gamster: gambler.

swoop-stake-like, draw at friend, and foe: as a gambler in a sweepstake, betting on all odds simultaneously; does Leartes want to destroy his friends as well as his enemies?

Endnotes

ope: open.

will: want.

forfor: presumably repetition through error.

sawe: saying; i.e. as transient as one of her father's maxims.

rew: rue, a herb associated with repentance.

hearb a grace: another name for rue.

dazie: daisy.

rosemary . . . For remembrance: the herb had a memorial significance. The 'remembrance' in question concerns both Corambis' and Ofelia's former selves.

pansey for thoughts: the flower is fancifully named from French *pensées*, 'thoughts'.

Page 87

document in madnes: a lesson in the logic of insanity.

they say the owle was / A Bakers daughter: refers to a folk-tale in which Christ was refused bread by a baker's daughter, and turned her into an owl.

For bonny sweete Robin . . .: popular song or group of songs.

sing a downe: refrain common in popular songs.

the false steward: reference to a lost folk-tale.

dan'd: donned.

dupt: contraction of 'do up', but here apparently meaning 'opened', perhaps by the lifting of a latch.

By gisse, and by saint Charitie: by Jesus and holy Charity.
bwy: contraction of 'God be with you'.

distracted: insane.

Page 88

unhearsed: i.e. once his wrath escapes from its tomb. The word echoes the Ghost's escape from its burial place, the event which began the first revenge cycle.

exeunt om.: *exeunt omnes*: all go out.

Endnotes

crossed by the contention: the ship was delayed by contrary winds.

his lookes: i.e. the King's.

commend me / A mothers care: communicate a mother's concern.

Be wary of his presence: look after himself.

in that . . .: in that which he's undertaking – i.e. revenge on the King.

fell not to his minde: have not turned out as he had hoped.

Page 89

that doome . . . poynted for him: the death sentence intended ('appointed') for himself.

thowsand: thousand.

let: hindrance.

My will, not all the world: by my will, nothing in the world will stand in my way.

Touching: concerning.

tasked: tempted.

try the maistry: attempt to win.

venies: venues, bouts or turns in fencing.

Page 90

singularitie: unique skill (i.e. in fencing).

lest that all should misse: if everything goes wrong.

period: the period of his life, i.e. his death.

heavily: sadly.

uncapable: incapable of understanding, unaware.

enter Clowne and an other: the second gravedigger, like the 'Centinels' in the opening scene, is referred to in speech prefixes only.

Page 91

Ergo: Latin, 'therefore'.

Y'are gone: you're beaten.

a great woman: a high-ranking lady.

Endnotes

stope: jar.

Mason: stonemason, builder.

his long home: i.e. death.

he throws up a shovel: there is no S.D. in Q2 and F at this point. Edward Capell emended Q1's direction in his edition (1767–8) to '*throws up a skull*'. Q1 may accurately direct or recall a dramatic action in which the Clown squats within the grave/trapdoor, with only his thrown-up shovel visible to indicate digging. The following conversation about skulls could easily be conducted without further props, the actors simply pointing into the grave. A respect for the textual evidence here throws up the intriguing possibility of a Jacobean Hamlet who never held a skull. Modern editions (including the Oxford 'original-spelling' edition) follow the eighteenth-century emendations.

ghest: guest.

joles: jolts, with a pun on 'jowl' = 'jaw'.

Page 92

mai't: may it.

indite . . . action of batterie: summons him on a charge of physical assault.

Quirkes and quillets: legalistic distinctions.

vouchers: the summoning of a third party to guarantee a holder's title to property. A double voucher involved two third parties.

leases and free-holde, / and tenements: terms from the vocabulary of property law.

conveiance: legal process of transferring property.

honor: perhaps simply 'the honourable man', or equivalent to 'your honour' addressed to a judge; but the word has also been deeply involved in legal vocabulary in the form of a range of technical phrases, one of which may be entailed here.

transformance: transformation.

Scull: skull.

the toe of the pesant . . . .: Hamlet has observed a process of social mobility in which the peasant approximates closely in rank to the courtier.

gawles his kibe: rubs his chilblain.

Endnotes

griound: ground.

pocky: poxy, diseased.

Page 93

parlous: perilous.

ground . . . ground: cause . . . territory.

powred: poured.

Rhenish: Rhine wine.

Alexander: Alexander the Great.

Page 94

boung: bung.

open fieldes: unconsecrated ground.

howling: i.e. in hell.

Forbeare the earth: delay covering the body with earth.

powre: pour.

Olympus: mountain home of the Greek gods.

Pellon: Pelion, another mountain in Thessaly. The Titans of Greek myth tried to scale heaven by piling one mountain onto another.

conjures: swears.

praiest: pray.

Page 95

doot: do it.

Oosell: possibly 'Ossa', another mountain involved in the Greek legend of the Titans.

A Cat will meaw . . .: Leartes (the cat) may 'whine', but Hamlet (the dog) will have his day.

tender: value.

exeunt omnes: all go out.

Page 96

water-flie: satirical image for an extravagant busybody.

Endnotes

The Court knowes him . . .: he is more notorious than respected in the Court.

foh: pooh!

muske-cod: the gland in a musk-deer secreting musk, used as a basis for making perfume.

embassage: message, diplomatic overture.

swoltery: sweltering.

carriages: straps for securing swords to the belt; a courtier's slang for 'hangers'.

girdles . . . hangers: belts . . . straps.

cosin german: closely related, appropriate.

canon by his side: the word 'carriage' sounds to Hamlet more like a gun-carriage than a hanger for a sword.

venies: venues, bouts or turns in fencing.

three oddes: three hits.

of the best judgement: the most discerning.

spiced: perfumed.

He will disclose himselfe without inquirie: you can smell him without asking for him / he tells you everything without being asked / his treachery is transparent, needing no interrogation.

Page 97

predestiuate providence: predestinate fate.

hane: have.

nature . . . honor: Leartes is personally willing to accept, but his obligations of honour prevent his acquiescence in Hamlet's offer of peace.

will no reconcilement: am not prepared to accept a reconciliation.

elder maisters: senior citizens (i.e. reliable judges).

foyles . . . foyle: fencing swords . . . material used to highlight something richer.

Have all a laught: are all of equal length.

tuch: touch.

bowt: bout.

Page 98

passe: pass, a fencing move.

cunningst play: cleverest skill.

keepe the gates: secure the gates.

coxcombe: fool.

Unbated: the point unprotected.

union: the King is united with his incestuous partner ('Gertred') and with his fate.

withall: in addition.

antike Roman: ancient Roman.

Page 99

draft: volley.

ambassie: message, diplomatic communication.

rearde: erected.

the State: the leading figures.

rights of memory: hereditary rights deriving from the past, i.e. to that portion of Denmark lost by his father to old Hamlet.

fieldes: i.e. battlefield.

Appendix

The Tragicall Historie of

HAMLET

Prince of Denmarke.

Enter two Centinels. { *now call'd Ber...*

1. STand: who is that?
2. Tis I.
1. O you come most carefully vpon your watch,
2. And if you meete *Marcellus* and *Horatio*,
The partners of my watch, bid them make haste.
1. I will: See who goes there.

    Enter Horatio and Marcellus.

Hor. Friends to this ground.
Mar. And leegemen to the Dane,
O farewell honest souldier, who hath releeued you?
1. *Barnardo* hath my place, giue you good night.
Mar. Holla, *Barnardo*.
2. Say, is *Horatio* there?
Hor. A peece of him.
2. Welcome *Horatio*, welcome good *Marcellus*.
Mar. What hath this thing appear'd againe to night.
2. I haue seene nothing.
Mar. *Horatio* sayes tis but our fantasie,
And wil not let beliefe take hold of him,
Touching this dreaded sight twice seene by vs;

      B   There-

Therefore I haue intreated him along with vs
To watch the minutes of this night,
That if againe this apparition come,
He may approoue our eyes, and speake to it.

    Hor. Tut, t'will not appeare.

    2. Sit downe I pray, and let vs once againe
Assaile your eares that are so fortified,
What we haue two nights seene.

    Hor. Wel, sit we downe, and let vs heare *Bermardo* speake
of this.

    2. Last night of al, when yonder starre that's west-
ward from the pole, had made his course to
Illumine that part of heauen, Where now it burnes,
The bell then towling one.

Enter Ghost.

    Mar. Breake off your talke, see where it comes againe.

    2. In the same figure like the King that's dead,

    Mar. Thou art a scholler, speake to it *Horatio.*

    2. Lookes it not like the king?

    Hor. Most like, it horrors mee with feare and wonder.

    2. It would be spoke to.

    Mar. Question it *Horatio.*

    Hor. What art thou that thus vsurps the state, in
Which the Maiestie of buried *Denmarke* did sometimes
Walke? By heauen I charge thee speake.

    Mar. It is offended.   *exit Ghost.*

    2. See, it stalkes away.

    Hor. Stay, speake, speake, by heauen I charge thee
speake.

    Mar. Tis gone and makes no answer.

    2. How now *Horatio*, you tremble and looke pale,
Is not this something more than fantasie?
What thinke you on't?

    Hor. Afore my God, I might not this beleeue, without
the sensible and true auouch of my owne eyes.

Mar.

[134]

Mar. Is it not like the King?

Hor. As thou art to thy felfe,
Such was the very armor he had on,
When he the ambitious *Norway* combated.
So frownd he once, when in an angry parle
He fmot the fleaded pollax on the yce,
Tis ftrange.

Mar. Thus twice before, and iump at this dead hower,
With Marfhall ftalke he paffed through our watch.

Hor. In what particular to worke, I know not,
But in the thought and fcope of my opinion,
This bodes fome ftrange eruption to the ftate.

Mar. Good, now fit downe, and tell me he that knowes
Why this fame ftrikt and moft obferuant watch,
So nightly toyles the fubieft of the land,
And why fuch dayly coft of brazen Cannon
And forraine marte, for implements of warre,
Why fuch impreffe of fhip-writes, whofe fore taske
Does not diuide the funday from the weeke:
What might be toward that this fweaty march
Doth make the night ioynt labourer with the day,
Who is't that can informe me?

Hor. Mary that can I, at leaft the whifper goes fo,
Our late King, who as you know was by Forten-
Braffe of *Norway*,
Thereto prickt on by a moft emulous caufe, dared to
The combate, in which our valiant *Hamlet*,
For fo this fide of our knowne world efteemed him,
Did flay this Fortenbraffe,
Who by a feale compaft well ratified, by law
And heraldrie, did forfeit with his life all thofe
His lands which he ftoode feazed of by the conqueror,
Againft the which a moity competent,
Was gaged by our King:
Now fir, yong Fortenbraffe,
Of inapproued mettle hot and full,

Hath

Hath in the skirts of *Norway* here and there,
Sharke vp a fight of lawleffe Refolutes
For food and diet to fome enterprife,
That hath a ftomacke in't : and this (I take it) is the
Chiefe head and ground of this our watch.

Enter the Ghoft.

But loe, behold, fee where it comes againe,
He croffe it, though it blaft me : ftay illufion,
If there be any good thing to be done,
That may doe eafe to thee, and grace to mee,
Speake to mee.
If thou art priuy to thy countries fate,
Which happly foreknowing may preuent, O fpeake to me,
Or if thou haft extorted in thy life,
Or hoorded treafure in the wombe of earth,
For which they fay you Spirites oft walke in death, fpeake
to me, ftay and fpeake, fpeake, ftoppe it *Marcellus.*

2.   Tis heere.   *exit Ghoft.*
Hor.   Tis heere.
Marc.   Tis gone, O we doe it wrong, being fo maiefti-
call, to offer it the fhew of violence,
For it is as the ayre invelmorable,
And our vaine blowes malitious mockery.
2.   It was about to fpeake when the Cocke crew.
Hor.   And then it faded like a guilty thing,
Vpon a fearefull fummons : I haue heard
The Cocke, that is the trumpet to the morning,
Doth with his earely and fhrill crowing throate,
Awake the god of day, and at his found,
Whether in earth or ayre, in fea or fire,
The ftrauagant and erring fpirite hies
To his confines, and of the trueth heereof
This prefent obiect made probation.
Marc.   It faded on the crowing of the Cocke,
Some fay, that euer gainft that feafon comes,
Wherein our Sauiours birth is celebrated,

The

[136]